The Pieces of You Tarot

Illuminating the Archetypes Within

Jim Larsen

Copyright © 2018 Jim Larsen
All rights reserved.
ISBN-978-0-9912920-9-7

This book is dedicated to everybody who has ever noticed that there is more to who we all are than meets the eye, and decided to look into that.

The images depicted here are based on a tarot card deck I bought while in China. This deck had no visible copyright information. I quite like the depiction of the archetypes of this deck, so I decided to use them to illustratie The Pieces of You Tarot: Illuminating the Archetypes Within.

Table of Contents

Introduction- 1
Major Archana- 5
The Fool- 6
The Magician- 9
The High Priestess- 12
The Empress- 15
The Emperor- 18
The Hierophant- 20
The Lovers- 23
The Chariot- 26
Strength- 29
The Hermit- 32
Wheel of Fortune- 35
Justice- 38
The Hanged Man- 40
Death- 43
Temperance- 45
The Devil- 47
The Tower- 50
The Star- 53
The Moon- 56
The Sun- 58
Judgment- 60
The World- 63
Swords- 67
Ace of Swords- 68
2 of Swords- 71
3 of Swords- 73
4 of Swords- 76
5 of Swords- 78
6 of Swords- 80

7 of Swords- 82
8 of Swords- 84
9 of Swords- 86
10 of Swords- 88
Page of Swords- 91
Knight of Swords- 93
Queen of Swords- 95
King of Swords- 97
Pentacles- 99
Ace of Pentacles- 100
2 of Pentacles- 102
3 of Pentacles- 104
4 of Pentacles- 106
5 of Pentacles- 108
6 of Pentacles- 110
7 of Pentacles- 112
8 of Pentacles- 114
9 of Pentacles- 116
10 of Pentacles- 117
Page of Pentacles- 120
Knight of Pentacles- 122
Queen of Pentacles- 124
King of Pentacles- 126
Wands- 128
Ace of Wands- 129
2 of Wands- 131
3 of Wands- 133
4 of Wands- 135
5 of Wands- 137
6 of Wands- 139
7 of Wands- 141
8 of Wands- 144
9 of Wands- 146
10 of Wands- 148
Page of Wands- 150
Knight of Wands- 152

Queen of Wands- 154
King of Wands- 156
Cups- 158
Ace of Cups- 159
2 of Cups- 162
3 of Cups-164
4 of Cups- 166
5. of Cups- 168
6 of Cups- 171
7 of Cups- 173
8 of Cups- 175
9 of Cups- 177
10 of Cups- 180
Page of Cups- 182
Knight of Cups- 185
Queen of Cups- 187
King of Cups- 189
In Conclusion- 192

Introduction

I don't care to use tarot cards to divine the future. I'll know the future when I catch up to it. The future never disappears. It's always just ahead, slightly out of reach. When we get there, we don't even notice it because suddenly it is "now." So what's the point of trying to figure it out when it's always changing anyway? Just relax and let it unfold as it will.

I prefer, instead, to use tarot cards to glean understandings of people. This includes myself. I have learned much about myself through tarot cards. I have learned what a Fool I am, willing to take leaps of faith that others will probably never understand. I have learned that I am a powerful Magician, able to draw to myself that which I desire, even when the odds of doing so are profoundly against me. I have learned that I am a Hermit whose Star shines brightly as I meditate and go within to find my talents, skills, and power. I have learned that am more King of Wands than King of Swords, as I am more passionate about my creative pursuits than my intellectual endeavors. I have come to appreciate the Three of Swords and the pain it carries without taking it personally. I have come to honor every aspect of myself as represented by the cards, and that is the purpose of this book, to encourage you to do the same.

Think about it. Every tarot card represents a piece of who we all are. When you understand all these pieces, you understand yourself. You understand others. You understand the human race, the human condition, and simple human nature. As you discover these aspects of yourself, so too will you see them reflected in others. You will start to notice their tarot personalities and what their dominate archetypes are, and in so doing, better predict what to expect from them.

A tarot card can remind you of an intrinsic quality that you possess. As you look at a card reflect on its qualities and see these resonating in yourself. For example, take a look at the Fool card. Consider the Fool's spontaneity and faith in itself. Consider its ability to take a leap of faith into some complete unknown, confident it will land on its feet, undaunted by the mystery of its new environment. Where in you do these qualities exist? Are they on the surface, or are they buried deep inside somewhere, forgotten or barely touched?

Consider the Strength card as another example. Where in yourself is the ability to face any challenge? Where is your ability to take on the weight of the world without being crushed by it? Where is your ability to endure attacks to your status-quo and your ego without taking it personally? These are qualities that sometimes need to be developed. How willing are you to work on them?

Take the Empress as one last example. Examine her ability to love and care for others without conditions. Do you judge those that you love for their faults and weaknesses, or do accept them as they are? Is it important for you to know that they are well provided for and that they have what they need to prosper? These are the hallmarks of a well developed inner Empress.

Don't expect every archetype to resonate with you. As you read this book, you may discover that some do not feel like a piece of you at all. You may ask yourself, "What is the author talking about? That's not me." This is to be expected. Some pieces of you are dormant. They have not been activated. To live the life you are meant to live, and to achieve what you are meant to achieve, the necessary aspects of your self have been ignited. These are the pieces of you that will carry you to where you need to be. The ones that remain dormant, while still a part of the overall you, are not essential to your life's mission, at least not yet. When needed, they will awaken. Chances are, you will experience at least a whisper of each during the course of your life.

To get the most from this book, read it with the intention of gleaning insights into yourself. Read it with the intention of gleaning insights into others. That is what this book is. It is a book of insights. It is meant to open windows to the multitude of personality types that exist in the human race. As you read this book, and as you delve into tarot with your own private practice, reflect on how each archetype is represented inside of yourself. Who do you know who exemplifies the essence of any particular archetype?

When somebody is a constant downer, you may say that this person is a real Nine of Swords, always looking for something to complain and cry about. Or, maybe you know somebody who is always happy and cheerful. You may say of them that they are a Three of Cups. You may also know somebody who is very inquisitive and always asking questions. You could say of them that they are a true Page of Swords. The list goes on.

For your own self, you may be going through a difficult time and are wondering how it will all turn out. In times like that, you may say you are having a Moon experience, and you can't wait for the cycle of the moon to turn so that you have clarity. You may be facing fears or dealing with buried emotions that have come to surface and are now causing you distress. In such times, you may say you are dealing with the Devil. You may be having the best day of your life, where you simply feel great and never want the day to end. During a day like that, you may say you enjoying your time in the Sun.

This is the beauty of tarot. It gives us a language by which to describe human nature in all its variations. It gives us metaphors to help us make sense of who, what, and how we all are. It reminds us of our oneness, our similarities and our differences. It lets us examine our strengths and our weaknesses. As you read this book, ask yourself which archetypes represent your strengths? Ask yourself too, which qualities would you like to develop? Once identified, you can begin the task of working on those.

The tarot is divided into two major types of cards known as the major and the minor arcana. You may be asking if there is a difference between the major arcana pieces of yourself and the minor arcana. The answer is, yes. Think of the pieces of yourself represented by the major arcana as your divine aspects. These are the pieces that are intrinsically tied to your life's purpose. They guide you through the obstacle course of your spirit's journey towards enlightenment. They steer you in the direction to where you need to be and keep you on track of what you should be doing to get the most out of your life.

The pieces of yourself represented by the minor arcana, on the other hand, represent your earthly, day to day life. These are your highs and lows, your joys and your disappointments, the fruits of your labor, the reaping of what you have sown, and the ideas and the inspirations that come your way. These are the building blocks of the content of your character, and the sum total of what life has made you. Your minor arcana pieces are what you become by both nature and nurture. The choices you make shape these aspects of yourself, as do your attitudes and beliefs. They are weakened and strengthened by how you handle yourself, relate to others, stand up to challenges, and appreciate the good things.

To see and appreciate tarot as pieces of yourself gives you power. You are taking control over your own destiny by strengthening those aspects of yourself that you feel will benefit you to strengthen, and to maybe back off some on those aspects of yourself that you feel are negative and keeping you from being the best you can be. To use tarot solely to divine your future is to deny the true power of tarot and your own true power as well. Create your own future. Do it by setting your intention on what you want, identifying and activating the piece of yourself that can help you get it, and going for it unrelentingly until you achieve it.

Part One: The Major Arcana

The pieces of ourselves related to our life purpose

THE FOOL

As a Fool, you must eventually make the decision to set out on your journey of self discovery. You must decide that the faith you have is equal to the energy needed to embark on a new quest. You must decide that the risks involved in leaving behind what is safe and secure is worth the payoff of accomplishment and arrival at the destination this journey is leading to. You must understand that no matter what, things will turn out fine. Even if you don't know how it will work out, just know it will. This gives you the courage to begin at all. This gives you the willpower to try.

The piece of you that is The Fool needs space to discover on its own what life is really about. This is the piece of you that can't be restricted, and it can't be stuck. It needs to spread its wings and fly. It needs to break free from those who impose inhibitions in order to figure out who it really is and to appreciate what is authentically important. How can this happen when it is concerned with what others think? It needs to break away to explore life, the universe, and the world without anybody slowing it down.

The Fool represents your deeply rooted need to be authentic, away from social conditioning and expectations. How can you be the real you when you are always around people who have set expectations of you? How can you express yourself freely and safely if you are always around people who only see you in set and specific ways? This keeps you in a box. How can you possibly find yourself this way? It just can't be done. The Fool is the piece of you that yearns to be authentic, yearns to be free, and yearns to explore.

One seldom discovers their true self in the place they have always been. One discovers their true self through exploration of the world beyond their familiar environment. When you are only surrounded by same, same, same familiarity, how can you possibly know what is pertinent and valuable to you? How do you know what is intrinsic and authentic to you? When what you know is all you know, how can you be sure there isn't more? The world is vast, and the universe is vaster. Explore the land, and explore your mind. Explore your spirit and explore your soul. These are the explorations that open the universe to you. By finding what the universe has for you, not only do you find your power, you find yourself.

To truly understand yourself, you need to get away from what is familiar to see how you react to the unfamiliar. You need to feel no sense of obligation to anybody or anything other than your own sense of adventure and need to explore and follow your own individual faith without the worries and projections of others casting a shadow over it. You need the freedom to go your own way on your own terms and to make the mistakes you need to make in order to learn the lessons they have for you. You are nothing without mistakes, so enable yourself to make them.

Without mistakes you may never examine your life and your circumstances and ask how to do better and get it right next time. Without mistakes, you would stagnate and become complacent. You would become lost in the hubris and believe yourself to be infallible. Sometimes you have to fall down so you can get back up and stand taller, firmer. Sometimes you have to be injured so you can heal stronger. Sometimes you have to fall behind so you develop the speed and agility to catch up. Sometimes you have to be abandoned so you can figure out where you are and where you want to be. So to create a paradigm in which you are free to explore on your own and to make mistakes without being judged for them by others or by yourself is to truly be on the path to personal power.

Once away from the familiar, what does it look like as you look back on it? Do you still see yourself there? Do you long to return, or do you want only to keep going? If you yearn to return, there is probably still a piece of you there. When you can, return and retrieve that piece. It will call to you until you do, and leave you with a sense of incompleteness. This is counterproductive to the actualization process. To be actualized, you must be complete, so leave no piece of yourself behind on your journey of self discovery.

As you return to the familiar, what has it become to you? Is it the same? If it is not, is it because you are not the same? What about your outlook and your attitude are different? How have your reactions to all that is familiar to you changed? In the context of your old familiarity, you will better understand the new you. You will recognize and appreciate the changes in yourself. You will appreciate just who you really are.

Being on this path to personal discovery is what it means to be a Fool. The Fool is that piece of you that is ready to take those leaps of faith that propel you on the journey to self authentication. This is the piece of you that feels the impulses to get away from the mundane familiarity of your world to see what else there is, and to see who else you are. This is the piece of you that walks with faith, even in darkness, knowing that you may stumble, but accepting that falling down and getting back up is all part of the journey. You have the strength to persevere and keep going.

A Fool's journey is not a singular occurrence. It is a continuous and ever-evolving event. The conclusion of one journey is the impetus of the next. Every time the Fool starts a new journey, he is that much stronger from the previous journey. This is true of the journeys within a life, and of journeys from lifetime to lifetime, from the mundane journeys of earthly life to the karmic journeys of our divine beings. This is the piece of you that is a Fool.

THE MAGICIAN

Manifestation is a raw, primal creative force. Where there was nothing, now there is something. From the simple desire for there to be, now there is. There is no such thing as nothingness, for even in complete silence, complete stillness, complete darkness, there is still energy vibrating. Where there is energy, there is a source. This source is a cause and a source of manifestation. This is a process in action. This raw vibration is the fundamental source of being. Even in silence, even in stillness, it is there. In the stillness of silence you can tap into this raw vibration of manifestation and shape it and bend it and form it to your needs and desires. When you know what it is, you own it. It is yours. As yours, it becomes what you need it to be.

This is the power of your inner Magician. You assess what is there as it pertains to what is needed. You tap into the powers of the universe and bring to the earth these things that will enhance your life and the world itself. You will reach those times when you realize that you want or need more out of life or out of a particular situation than you are getting, and endeavor to do something about it. You set the intention to bring into being what you really want.

The first step towards actualization is getting clear and understanding exactly what it is that you want. If you are not exactly clear on what you are trying to achieve, how will you know that you achieved it? Ambiguous intentions lead to ambiguous results, leaving you with little choice but to hope for the best with what you end up with. Is this truly what you want?

Does this truly provide what you need? If not, try again, and this time create a very clear intention on what you want.

The piece of you that is the Magician is not passive. This piece of you is active and insightful. It does not wait for something to happen. It does not assess situations to see what is needed just so to sit back and wait for it to be actualized. The Magician, having ascertained what is needed, brings it into being. It actively sets in motion the events that bring forth the manifestation of this thing. This is the true power of your inner Magician.

Your inner Magician uses what it sees to create wisdom. How does the Magician know what is needed? It can only do this by having knowledge of the whole. The Magician is a holistic seer. It delves deep, beyond the surface. It sees the inner working, the fundamental intrinsic nature of a situation and is aware of every component. The Magician piece of you, in this way, has tremendous awareness. This awareness enables it to see the missing pieces. Once seen, it knows what to manifest, and does so by looking at the blank space where something should be, and filling it with the energy of that thing until it is there.

If you find it difficult to activate the Magician piece of you, remember, you create your reality with your beliefs. This is because what you believe is real to you. If you see yourself as poor, you will be poor. If you see yourself as rich, you will be rich. If you see yourself as healthy, wealthy, wise, competent, incompetent, able, unable, willing, unwilling, anything, this is what you will be. So see yourself as the greatest emanation of yourself, allowing no one to degrade this view. For how you see yourself is what you believe about yourself, so this is what you will become. You create your own life. You create your own miracles. You create your own reality. This is true of the circumstances of your inner life, and of your outer environment.

In that our thoughts create our reality, so too does it create our health. When symptoms arise, do you focus on what is "wrong" with yourself, thus drawing more and more attention to it and causing it to grow, or do you focus on eliminating the symptoms, perhaps visualizing golden and white light radiating towards it? Do you put forth the energy of sustaining the symptoms or the energy of eliminating them? The choice is our own, and you will accomplish what your mind sets out to.

Your inner Magician is an innovator. This gives you the ability to transcend what is simple and earthly to see the possibilities of what is available. It gives you the skills to put elements together in a new way to create a new paradigm altogether. Your inner Magician is acutely tuned into the environment and knows the value of all that is present, and can thus identify what is missing. It looks into the divine realms to create on earth. Your inner Magician is always open to inspiration. It looks for it everywhere. The piece of you that is a Magician is an inventor and an artist of the earth. It listens to the voices and feels the impulses, and it responds. You inner Magician is the door on the earth through which divinity is received.

THE HIGH PRIESTESS

The High Priestess confidently knows the truth. There is no room for doubt here. There is no reason to question. The High Priestess is speaking to you, and her words are truthful. She is that voice in your head that whispers, telling you truths you may otherwise be blind to. Not blind as in unable to see, but blind as in unwilling to see. She is the voice of your intuition, your gut feeling personified. Her messages are astute and profound. To listen or to not listen is completely up to you. To listen is to be granted wisdom that will serve you well. To not listen is to deprive yourself of insights that will benefit you greatly. Listen to the High Priestess when she whispers, and you will be granted wisdom beyond the mundane.

Your High Priestess has the unique and enviable ability to be far-seeing and wide-seeing. She is the piece of you that knows the absolute truth with confidence, her perceptions going beyond the mundaneness of a situation or concern. She sees holistically, both the pettiness and the importance of it all. Where others close their eyes, the High Priestess is only just starting to see. She has no concern for the ego, but rather operates completely outside of the paradigm that the ego creates. The ego sets limits, but the High Priestess is limitless. She will not be hindered by prejudices, preconceived notions, or limiting beliefs. She will speak. Tune your ear beyond the static and the noise to hear.

The High Priestess may tell you things that you do not want to know, but that does not mean you don't need to hear it. Listen to the voice of the

High Priestess. Her words are never arbitrary. Quiet your ego so she does not have to scream to be heard. She will speak no matter what. Can you hear her? Will you listen to what she says? She does not care one way or the other what you want to hear. Her job is to tell you what is pertinent and what is necessary.

The High Priestess reminds you that you know. You know, but maybe you just don't want to admit that you know. Maybe the truth that you know is not the truth you want to face. But realize this- just because you don't want to face it, it's not going to change or go away, so you might as well accept it. It happens like that sometimes, your gut will tell you something you don't want to face because it is too painful. Painful or not though, it is real, so deal with it head on. The truth cannot be altered or diminished, no matter what that truth represents to you- be it joy, pain, or simple indifference. None of that matters.

What matters is that it will not go away just because you don't like it. You can deny it, you can hide from it, you can even convince your self that it is not real. When you do this, all it will do is fester within and resurface later as an un-dealt with issue in your life where you will have another chance to deal with it then. So why not deal with the truth, whatever it is right now, so you don't have to deal with it later? Remember, the High Priestess always deals with the absolute truth. She represents pure guidance from the universe that is unspoiled by the ego and desire. It is just simply real.

How does the High Priestess know what she knows? What is her source of wisdom? Pure intuition is a holistic knowing. One cannot be purely in tune with this holistic knowing if they are focused on the ego, for the ego is centered on the "I" in wholeness. While "I" is a component of wholeness, it is not the center of it all nor is it the driving force, although the ego acts like it is. As long as the ego takes this attitude, it will never be completely open to the absolute truth of pure intuition, for as long as the ego is involved, it will always endeavor to know how the situation pertains to it more so than the wholeness. The High Priestess, however, is adept at setting the ego aside and not accepting it all, focusing instead on the holistic nature of the universe and understanding the situation at hand as it fits into it.

What is your gut instinct telling you? Is it something good? Is it something to get excited about? If so, look forward to it! You know to trust your gut feelings. If you feel like something good is coming your way, you know it's for real and you can anticipate this with a good feeling. But does your gut give you a bad feeling? Is this that you are anticipating something you wish you didn't have to deal with? If so, as you wait for it, mentally prepare for it. Chances are you can't change the event that is coming your way, but you can change your feelings about it. Visualize yourself getting through it before it happens and it will be that much easier to deal with.

The High Priestess piece of you gives you the ability to know the truth with confidence, to not doubt yourself, and to know the truth without questioning it. This is your voice of intuition, and intuition is pure and perfect.

THE EMPRESS

Imagine what would happen if you opened your heart fully and expressed all the love you feel without inhibition or fear. You would be a super-being who makes an incredible difference in the lives of others, for who doesn't need love and understanding? The truth is, you do have this ability. You absolutely can open your heart to express the love that is in there. You just need to find the courage to do it. This is easy to do when that love is returned, but can you do it even when it is not? Can you express all the love you have for somebody even when they don't mirror it back to you? That piece inside of you that has love, compassion, understanding, concern, and genuine empathy for others is The Empress, and it is able to express these things without placing conditions on them. Maybe these will be reflected back, maybe they won't be. It is no matter. What matters is the wellbeing of those you care about, and that you keep this in your awareness.

Consider the mothering qualities of The Empress. She has a loving nature and nurturing tendencies. Now ask yourself, who in your life could benefit from these qualities from you? Is there somebody who is feeling low, who could really use a friend? What can you do for this person, or these people? Do not be blind to the people who could really use a little of that magic you offer. If this is somebody you are comfortable giving a hug, give them a hug. If this is somebody you can make laugh, make them laugh. If this is somebody to whom you are comfortable saying, "I love you," then say "I love you."

There are going to be those who could use your understanding, love, and support. Don't hesitate to give it to them. We all need these things ourselves every so often, so when somebody in your life needs it too, why hold back? Who among us doesn't go through some time where we need to just fall apart even a little? We all need to fall apart so we can rebuild sometimes. In falling apart, we may not project our optimal self. We may be difficult to be around. We may seem out of control or unlikable. Nobody is immune to this, and when we are going through this, doesn't it help to have some understanding and compassion? It is the same for the people in your life. Give them the space and acceptance they need to rebuild their selves into the best person they can be. This is what a true Empress would do. Give love, but give space too. It makes all the difference.

The Empress, with her ability to nurture and promote life, will naturally have a view and an understanding of what life is and what it can be. She will then help to provide that which is needed to promote the growth and sustainability of this life, for herself and others. She will promote the establishment of roots for those she cares about, so that they will grow strong on their own with a firm foundation.

The Empress piece of you reminds you that what seed you plant is what will grow, and what you project, is what will be returned. Imagine that the words you speak, the actions you take, and your attitude you have towards others bounce back to you as if they hit a mirror. What then, do you want this reflection to be? Consider this when you interact with people. Would you rather have heaviness and negativity coming back to you, or lightness and affirmations?

It is true also that your words, actions, and attitudes towards others will sink into their heart and influence their feelings and their mood. This will no doubt play a role in their own interactions with people. Why not plant seeds of light and harmony in the hearts of others so that they will spread it to others? When speaking to somebody, why not aim high? Aim to inspire, not to deflate. Negative words make people shrink, to shrivel up. Their light becomes walled in. They must struggle now to let their light out again. Imagine how much better you would feel knowing you helped them shine their light?

The power of The Empress is the power to create new life and new ideas. The Empress holds within her the essence of new creation. She holds it until it is ready to be given to the world. She has impeccable timing. She knows exactly when this new creation is ready for the world. Once in the world, the Empress has the power to nurture it and help it to grow. The power of the Empress is to see within others, their unique talents, abilities, essence, and how to nurture them. She has the ability to anticipate and intuit the needs of the people she cares about, and then to provide this. The Empress quality within you cares deeply about the wellbeing of others, and will tap into the potential of others to bring to fruition their greatest potential.

THE EMPEROR

The Emperor is characterized by the ability to take a stand, to root in firmly and not be swayed by distractions. The power of the Emperor piece within you is to know and appreciate your own strengths and to let them form a strong foundation from which you exercise your power. This does not, however, mean to operate so firmly that you push away and neglect the needs and opinions of others. It does not mean to be such a dominating force of nature that you become lost in the hubris, believing too much in your own importance.

You cannot reason with a force of nature, and any attempts to will lead to frustration. The wind is going to blow no matter what. The rain is going to rain and the snow is going to fall. You have no power to stop or influence them. The tides will come in and go out without concern to your desires. There is simply no reasoning with any of it. All you can do is react to it all and make necessary preparations. This can be the same with people. They can be set in their ways, unwilling to change or bend the rules they live by even the slightest for anybody's benefit. They can be stubborn. They can be ornery. They can be so trapped in their boxes of rigid beliefs that trying to reason with them will only frustrate you. What can do but conform your own self around their stubbornness and deal with your frustration the best you know how?

When considering the qualities of a true leader, a true Emperor, this force of nature approach does nobody any good. A true leader, a true authority or father figure must not be so fixated on their own interests that they alienate those who rely on their guidance. They must be open to the ideas and needs of those who depend on them without being so absorbed in their own way of doing things. Otherwise, what happens? What growth ever transpires? While at times they may have a legitimate sense of what is best for the group, taking the approach that their ideas are infallible based solely on their position as "leader" can lead to a lot of bad ideas being perpetrated. This accomplishes nothing but to drag the group down.

The piece of you that is the Emperor, in its best sense, while able to root in, remain firm, and take a stand, is also able to reason. It is not an absolute dictator. It is a leader who is able to listen to others and appreciate their needs and viewpoints. This is the piece of you that is willing to hear somebody out and take their concerns into consideration when making decisions that will affect an entire group. This is the piece of you that is able to admit when they are wrong, or that somebody else has a better idea. This is the piece of you that can take constructive criticism without getting upset over it. These are the hallmarks of a strong leader. To be the strongest Emperor you can be, practice all of this. Practice listening to others and being cognizant of their perspectives and needs.

Strong leaders are revered and appreciated for their ability to hold the vision for the group and guide them towards the actualization of that vision. They are the central point through which the ideas and opinions of the group go through to be actualized. They weigh the ideas and concerns of all and filter what is pertinent from what does not fit with a genuine concern for the feelings of those whose ideas may have to be shot down because they do not fit the vision. They are not so full of their self that they have to always be right. They are though, strong enough to stand up for their own ideas and weave them into those of others until there is a solid plan that fits the situation at hand. This is the piece of you that is the Emperor. Focus on it, and make it strong.

THE HIEROPHANT

Whether you realize it or not, people look up to you. They see you as wise. You know things they wish they did, and you have life experience that they are still amassing. They see you as worldly and astute. This is the piece of you that is the Hierophant. Your inner Hierophant is a teacher. This is the piece of you that is able to share what you know in a concise and to the point manner. Your inner Hierophant is the holder of wisdom, and wisdom is legacy. To share your wisdom is to immortalize your existence. In this way, the Hierophant within you will live forever.

Consider the questions that people ask you. These are questions that only a learned, wise, and knowledgeable person could answer. The fact that you are the one being asked these questions, and the fact that you actually have the answers should tell you just how much you really do know. Did you know you knew this much? Sometimes you don't realize how far you have come on our path of wisdom until you get these little reminders. How others see you can tell us a lot about who you are. When they seek to know what you know, you know that what you have inside is valuable. You know that it is not for nothing to have this knowledge, for if it was for nothing, it would not be sought by others.

The job of your inner Hierophant is to facilitate success. Success is not in only what you achieve for yourself, but in how you influence others to achieve their success as well. What doors can you open for them? What lights can you lead them to? What wisdom can you share that will benefit their advancement? The knowledge you share becomes the scaffolding they use to build their own understandings. Take this seriously and be honored by it. Don't betray it with knowingly false information or outright lies. Let knowledge be sacred. Otherwise what's it's value? If they are building on a scaffolding of deception, how strong will their knowledge be? If their knowledge is weak, what does this say of you, the one who was expected to teach them well?

There are different ways to be a Hierophant and share what you know. You can teach by answering questions that people ask you. You can lecture. You can write books, articles, essays, and letters to the editor. You can tweet, blog, share something worth sharing on Facebook. If you're not worried about legalities, you can even grab a can of spray point and write something worthwhile on the side of a train for people to read as it goes by. That is not recommended, but if you are an artist, why not embed wisdom in some thought provoking images? If you're poetic, embed it in a poem. Write something that will make somebody ask, "What does that mean?" As they search for the answer, there will be much for them to learn. Instigate that. Instigate it with your creative powers. Create something for the world that will prompt thought and discussion.

Knowledge is power. So is wisdom. We each possess both based on our individual life paths, experiences, and expectations. Knowledge is to have education; wisdom is to have experience. To be a Hierophant means to be truly aware of what these things intrinsically mean. To be acutely aware of what you know and what you can do with what you know is to live a fulfilled life. Others will notice this. They will tap into your knowledge and wisdom for their own personal needs and growth. As a keeper of this knowledge and wisdom, you are in a unique position to shape their lives. Take this seriously. Honor those who ask you for these lessons of life by giving them serious and well articulated answers. They look to you as the wise guru of your family, community, school, office, carpool, or whatever the setting is where people ask you for answers. Live up to that expectation by taking their quest for answers seriously.

Your inner Hierophant, for its own sake, will never stop seeking answers to the many questions the world and the universe presents. Life is a constant quest for new wisdom, knowledge, and information. Those whose think they know everything are severely stagnating their selves. They are severely limiting any future growth and progress that they could be enjoying. This is not the way of a Hierophant. No, your true inner Hierophant will forever be on a quest to learn more. It will continually ask questions and seek answers. It will always share what it knows with anybody who needs to hear it. Your inner Hierophant will never die.

THE LOVERS

We feel love for a person when they allow us to be the best version of our self. They trigger us in a positive way. Those qualities that are natural to us, they amplify what we naturally feel. This turns to joy. This feeling of joy is interpreted as love. We have in us, that quality that both triggers others, and is triggered in ourselves by certain individuals. This is the piece of ourselves that is The Lovers.

There is no one perfect definition for "love." Everybody who has ever felt it will give you a different description of it. And it is a good guess that we have all felt it, which means there are a lot of different things to say about it. Maybe love is a general sense that the world is a better place with a certain other being in it, and you want to experience the world more and more within the paradigm of that being. In this way, love is attached to "I." "I like how I feel with this person in my life. I don't want this feeling to ever end." Here, love is as it is attached to the feeler of the love. In a perfect sense, this is not about the ego; this is not an obsession. In a perfect sense, this is attached to the heart. The heart likes the feeling of having this other person in its life.

Love can also be as it is attached to the recipient of the love. It can be a concern for the well-being of others when you know that all you will receive in return is the knowledge that their life is that much better, and the good feeling that gives you. With this in mind, maybe the best way to show love for others and love for the world is just to do deeds, both grand and small, to benefit others and the world with no expectation of anything concrete coming back to you. By attaching no expectations to what you will get back for your actions, what comes back to you will be pure, perfect, and exactly what you need to fill your heart.

The piece of you that is The Lovers desires a harmonious flow of energy between itself and the piece that is The Lovers in the one it loves, where one is not too overbearing and the other is not too possessive. The flow between the two is perfect for who the two are. Both are equally secure. There is no insecurity here as you are both equally giving and receiving.

The goal, perhaps, is to establish "one heart" where there is no separation between what is in your heart and what is in the other's heart. There is no separation because there are no boundaries between the two. The joining together is completely seamless. You are free to enter, with the other having no fear of what you will bring or of who will follow. You are free to enter without fear of what you will find. You are free to enter without a fear that you are unwanted or do not belong. You are free to enter without the worry that you will disturb what is there or be attacked as a trespasser. One heart where both belong: when the love you feel for another is strong, this is the desire.

Love can be to forge a trust that you know beyond any limitations of doubt will not be broken. Trust, though, can be a slippery concept. It may require an occasional recalibration as those contracted to it will experience their own personal growth, evolution, and awakenings separate from the contract of trust. Trust must be entered into with the understanding that it may at times be bent to test its agility and strength. When bent, true trust will regain its original position without breaking.

Trust, like all other things, is a perception. What you perceive as betrayal may to another be nothing of the sort. It may be a matter of living moment to moment. To you, this moment should mean one thing. To the other, it means something else. If your perception of the moment is not in alignment with one another's it may seem that trust has been broken. Before reacting, communicate. Be sure that each of you understands the motivations, feelings, and perceptions of the other. When trust is strong, this should happen naturally. If trust is not strong, how certain is the love?

The piece of you that is The Lovers, is willing to put the needs of others ahead of its own. It is open to the needs and viewpoints of others, and genuinely cares about them even when it may have to sacrifice its own needs for that of another. It's heart is open and honest in a relationship as it develops an intuition that benefits the other. This piece of you maintains a sense of self in a relationship, yet is unified in partnership.

THE CHARIOT

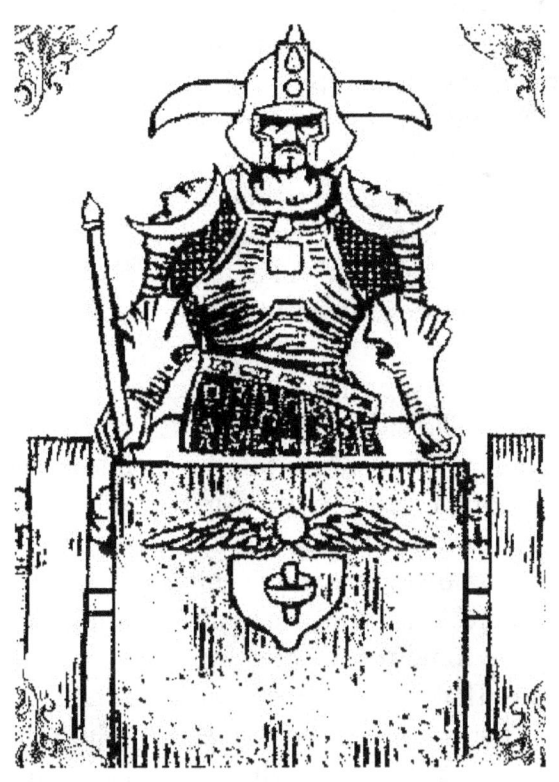

It is so easy to sit around and think about all the great and wonderful things you will do one day. To stop thinking and actually do them though, takes effort and motivation. Do you want to be one of those people who does nothing but talk? No! You don't! You want to be somebody who accomplishes things! So get up and get busy! Motivate yourself! Get things done! Pick a goal- any goal. Now ask yourself, what needs to happen to make this goal happen? Make a list if that helps. What is the first thing to do? Do it! What is something you can't do until a bunch of other things get done first? Do those other things so you can get to it! Don't just dream. Dreams are great to realize your possibilities, but dreaming is only the first step in the process of achievement. Actually doing the work is what propels you to your goals. So dream, visualize, and DO! This desire to achieve is the piece of you that is The Chariot.

People often speak of figuring out their life. This is well and good, but these people are thinking way too much about it. The one true trick to figuring out your life is to make a decision about doing something and sticking to it. Your life is going to go in a new direction no matter what decision you make, so pick a direction and go. Whatever direction you decide, you can make adjustments and alterations to the course once you have movement and gather momentum. So get this movement started so you can see the adjustments that need to be made. It's that simple. So when considering such things, remember you can take control of your own life, and make the decisions that propel it in the direction you want it to go. All you need to provide is the motivation. Tap into your inner Chariot and

DO IT!

The piece of you that is the Chariot craves freedom and independence. This is the piece of you that will not be slowed down by fences, gates, barriers or obstacles. When a fence, gate, barrier, or obstacle appears, you laugh at it. You put your dreams into hyperdrive and either crash through or fly over them. Who has time for obstacles? Life is for the living, and you are alive! No time to slow down to appease the gatekeepers. No time to be what others expect you to be. No time to be held back. You have ambition. You have power. You have talent. You have a vision. Nothing will deter you from reaching your goals as long as you remain focused on them.

When others only dream, you do. What others wish for, you achieve. When others give up, you are just getting started. And why is this? It's because you have the fortitude to follow through. You don't quit in the middle. You don't drop out. When the going gets tough, you don't give up because it got too hard or you're afraid. You see beyond obstacles to the open vistas beyond it. You are not distracted. You know where you're going and you are not going to stop until you get there. You know what you are doing and you are not going to stop until you are done. You are creating and you are not going to stop until it is complete. That is how you get things done. This is how you achieve your greatness. That is how you do things that others do not, simply by setting your goals, setting into motion what you must do to achieve those goals, and by not making excuses and quitting when it gets difficult.

The power of The Chariot is the freedom and independence it brings. This is the true essence- the core- of who you are. This is you unrestricted and unbridled. This is who you are when you are not slowing yourself down to accommodate anybody. This is who you are without any extra weight on you. This is you when you are not bound by the quirks, rules, and idiosyncrasies of others. This is you flying by the gatekeepers of your dreams and ambitions to achieve what you want to achieve and what you find important. You are unrestricted and the limits others live by and try to place on you are seen for what they are: arbitrary and pointless. Do the limits others place on you contribute to your overall well-being, or do they keep the status-quo of the person who is imposing them? Crash through the gates. Always. Don't let the gatekeepers hold you back.

By the force of your own power, achieve! The Chariot is saying to you, "Hey! Don't sit there waiting for somebody to tell what you can and what you should do. You know the answers, and you know how to do it. So do it!" It's so easy to slip into a thought system where you believe that you need to do things that other people want from you. It is easy to take their instructions and do your duties. You do it at work, you do it in relationships, you watch TV and buy what the commercials tell us to buy. But there is a flip side to that. There is also what you yourself are capable of doing without the need for anybody else telling you what to do. This is your creative genius side. This is your entrepreneurial side. This is your adventurous and independent side. This is your inner Chariot. Tap into it and get things done! No Excuses!

STRENGTH

The piece of you that is Strength has a strong sense of the totality of you. It knows the optimized version of who you are, and it knows what triggers you. It knows your passions and it knows what you find vile. It knows your worldview and it knows your comfort zone. It knows your weaknesses and it knows what makes you tick. This is the piece of you that has its finger on the pulse of your spirit to keep you acceptably balanced, and it provides the necessary impulses to keep you on an even keel.

When something or somebody bothers you, or irritates you, or triggers you, do you fly off the handle and make a scene about it? You probably do, sometimes, and that's okay. Try not to make that your normal response though. Try to stay calm and approach the situation with a rational mind. Find the Strength within to endure. You may need to speak up, of course. You may need to stand up for yourself or another. When you do have to, do so. But maintain control. Maintain order. Don't let the situation descend into chaos. If the situation involves another person, don't let it become a clash of egos.

Meeting ego with ego is seldom productive. Meet ego with contemplation. When the blunt force of somebody's ego charges at you, step aside and let it go by. If you do not let it sink into you, it has no place to go and is therefore neutralized. If you let it sink in, it gains power. It will grow stronger, more intense, and even harder to deal with. Now your triggers are magnified. They are in charge. They have power over you. Why let that happen? Instead, maintain a rational mind. Don't let anybody's attitude become your problem. Tap into your strength.

Sometimes you may be bothered by somebody, and there is no real detectable reason for it; there is just something about them that bothers you. When this happens, examine what it is that bothers you. It's not on the surface, so dig deep to find it. When feeling bothered, ask yourself why. "Why is this person bothering me? What is it about him or her?" What you find is your strength, and what it is that bothers you is your ego's perception of attack against this strength. It can feel like a battering ram is pounding at your heart's core.

It's as if you have built your life on the principle that this strength is important, but to this person, it is nothing. How will it change your existence if this person is right? What if what you find important is actually pointless? Let that idea float through you, then remind yourself that what is intrinsic to you, your core values and integrity cannot be attacked or altered without your consent. This person cannot affect you unless you let them, so it is okay to let your guard down and not feel threatened. He or she are who he or she is, and they have every right to be. You are who you are, and you too have every right to be. Then just let it go.

The piece of you that is Strength may ask you to consider how you handle unpleasant situations that come your way. It is normal, sure, to feel overwhelmed by the energy of a person, or of people, or of a place or situation. And sure, this can make you want to shrink away and hide to avoid it all to begin with. But the thing is, the world is not going to change to fit your needs. The world is not going to change just to be something you are comfortable with or comfortable in. Therefore, true strength is to create mechanisms and strategies to deal with and cope with all the energy you feel coming at you without being bowled over by it. Find ways to defeat it. Find ways to stay grounded. Find ways not to let any of it get to you. When you can this, you will be powerful. When you can do this, you are the master of your circumstances, not a victim of that which you find unpleasant. In this way, you become powerful. Be powerful.

When you are strong, do you really need to work so hard to prove anything to anybody? When you are strong, isn't it enough to use your strength when and how needed? Do you really have to show off and brag about it? True strength is the strength to be yourself, whatever that may be and however you define it. True strength is to give your strength to others when they need it, however they need it. This could be the strength to stand up for an underdog, to protect those who need to be protected, to be the rock somebody needs or to be the shoulder to cry on. This is the strength to accept others without judgment, help them through the rough times, and celebrate the good times with them. This is the strength to let somebody know you care about them, and that they are not alone when they are not feeling good about their self.

What would happen if instead of putting each other down, projecting our egos onto each other, suppressing each other and making each other feel bad, we instead lifted and enlightened each other? When you feel belittled and made small by another, uplift yourself by inspiring and uplifting somebody else. Generate an inspirational ripple this way. This is to use your Strength to inspire and put some good out into he world.

THE HERMIT

Drop out of society.
Society is boring anyway. Society is but a conglomeration of everybody else's ideas about how life ought to be lived. Break away from that. Paddle your own canoe. Go where you want to go. Get away from the group. Think your own thoughts. Group think roots you into the group. Do you want to be a part of the group? What's so great about the group? As long as you agree with everything the group is thinking, saying, and wanting, sure, you'll fit right in. Think your own thoughts though, and then see what happens. Speak your mind and want your own wants, and suddenly you're an outcast. Express a sentiment that is incongruent with the group thought and risk banishment. Sure, stay with the group and see how appreciated your individualism is. The piece of you that is The Hermit has had enough of all that. The piece of you that is The Hermit needs to think its own thoughts and express its own spirit.

The Hermit in you needs to break away and reflect inward. It can't always be concerned with what everybody else needs or expects from it. This piece of you needs to be a rock on its own merit, not a grain of sand in a committee of millions of others grains of sand that are all the same. Instead of living life by committee, look inside of your self and find the bits and pieces that add up to what you really want and really need.

In society, you're expected to please people and be what they want you to be. But that is ridiculous. Live your own life. Do your own thing, and those of a like mind will find you. As a Hermit, lead the way without looking in the rear view mirror. Be the leader, but do it quietly. Don't shout your demands and your beliefs. Whisper them. See who hears. See who follows. See who catches up to you. These are the people whose lives you are meant to affect, and you know this because they found you. You didn't go out looking for them. They were drawn to you based on what you have to offer. You are the ideal they will endeavor to live up to.

The Hermit within you knows its own wisdom. It values the silence and stillness in which it is found. It appreciates the conditions in which the lessons of life are learned, even when these conditions are painful. It doesn't put up walls against inspiration or deny a teacher of its own. It has no use for superfluous utterings or pointless small talk, knowing that the mass of humanity would seem so much smarter if they simply didn't talk so much.

Your inner Hermit is a quiet, secure person who doesn't feel the need to vocalize everything that pops into its head, and thus presents itself as intelligent. Those who speak each and every mundane thing that comes to mind so often come across as having questionable intelligence. Where in all that they are saying is anything useful? If they are just going on about how cute a kitten is or how their favorite sports team is doing this season, how seriously are they going to be taken? Who is still going to be listening if they actually do say something of value?

You're inner Hermit knows better than to fall into that trap. Why say these things if they are not relevant to the situation or the conversation? Who cares how cute that kitten is? Yes! We can all see it. Why does it need to be said? Cute kitten. Whatever. And what difference does it make how such and such a sports team is doing? There is no reason to interject that into a conversation that has nothing to do with that. So, to generate an appreciation for its intelligence, your Hermit within endeavors to keep its thoughts to itself unless they are of value in the moment, or saved for later when they are pertinent. Your inner Hermit is the personification of deep wisdom. In its capacity as one who is comfortable in its own skin without the need to overtly impress anybody, it is also the personification of self confidence.

Your inner Hermit is comfortable spending time alone. It doesn't need the constant attention of others, and can find an appropriate balance between alone time and time with others. It finds the answers it is looking for by going within. The piece of you that is The Hermit is your own private guru.

Honor it as such, and the wisdom of the universe will be available to you.

WHEEL OF FORTUNE

Those with a strong sense of personal fortune show appreciation for what they have. They understand the value of what is at hand. They appreciate what materials can be used for beyond the obvious, such as in recycling and composting. They have the ability to generate an abundance and know what to do with it all. They do not let things go to waste, and they know how to make the most of everything. They are not stingy, and are frugal only when it is important to be so. They appreciate money as energy and they keep it flowing. This is your inner Wheel of Fortune excerting its influence.

For some, having an excess of what they need- having more and more and more of something, be it money, gold, candy, friends, loved ones, whatever it is equates to having a fortune. For others having a fortune may mean simply having all they need of the various things they require without that need for more and more and more. What fortune is to you, that is what fortune is to you. What fortune is to me, that is what fortune is to me. Ask anybody what fortune means to them, and every one of them will give a different answer. The piece of you that is the Wheel of Fortune is the piece of you that knows what you need to survive, and what you need to be happy. This is the piece of you that will define your idea of Fortune.

Ask yourself, "I am happy, right? I have what I need, right?" If the answer is an honest "No, not really." Do not use this as an excuse to be a martyr. Assess what is positive and good in your life and make a realistic plan to fill in the gaps with what you truly honestly need. Whatever you do, don't whine or complain that things are not perfect, because you yourself have the ability to make it perfect. Whining and complaining does nothing but put your woes under a magnifying glass and augments them. It makes them so much more visible to the world and makes you seem weak. When filling in these gaps, start with your attitude and go from there. Fortune will follow.

If the answer to "I am happy, right? I have what I need, right?" is "Yes. I really am happy." Take inventory of what this happiness consists of. When times get tough you will want to remember what makes your life good. You'll want to remember where it is within you so you know where to find it when dark clouds obscure your perception of it. Take inventory and enjoy what you find. Appreciation for the joys of your life will augment them. Feeling good about what makes you feel good will create a chain reaction of joy until you can't believe just how much greatness you have.

Take inventory of your fortune without comparing it to the fortune of another, if you can. This can be hard to do because it's so easy to use what somebody else has or what they lack as a gauge to measure what we ourselves have. When you stop comparing yourself to others though, you can get a picture of just how fortunate you are. You might feel good because you have more than them. You might feel bad because you have less. See if you can you train yourself not to do that, and appreciate what you have that enhances the quality of your life without regard for how others measure up. When you examine what you have, you will likely discover there are things you would like to have but don't. Let this stand on its own merit, not a merit based on comparison. Let the notion of fortune be a personal matter. Let it exist as it is pertinent to you intrinsically, not egotistically.

If you have one hundred dollars, do you wonder why you don't have two hundred? How about a million? Do you wonder why you don't have a million dollars, even if one hundred is enough? Did you put in the work to earn a million dollars? If you didn't, that's your reason for not having it. If you are eating a hamburger too, do you wonder why you don't have a steak? If you have water to drink, do you wonder why you don't have orange juice? Some people live their life this way. No matter what, there is a lack of contentment. They continually feel like something is wrong because in their mind, they don't have what they "need." But if they relaxed and stopped worrying about what they don't have and examined the good qualities of what they do have, they would surely see that their life is good regardless of what isn't there. They will see that sure, a steak would be great, but the hamburger they are eating is just fine, and the water they are drinking is perfect.

The power of your inner Wheel of Fortune is in knowing what you want and assessing what you have, then honestly taking a look at what you need. When you have everything you need, you feel good about it. When you have everything you want, you feel even better. When you sense that something is missing though, you may feel that your life is out of kilter. So you endeavor to fill in what is missing so as not to have gaps. When these gaps are filled, you will feel fortunate.

JUSTICE

There is a piece within you that delights in seeing things work out the way they should. This piece likes to see people get what they deserve, whether it is a positive reward for good deeds, or punishment for bad. This same piece of you will stand up for underdogs to make sure they are treated fairly. This piece will also stand up for you and won't let you be used or treated like a doormat. This piece of you is Justice.

Justice is to be fair equitable. This is to not show favoritism, or let your decisions be swayed by emotion. This is to apply logic and clear, levelheaded thinking to all situations. The Justice piece of you will settle for nothing less than honesty. The minute untruths seep into a situation, this is the piece of you that will sound the alarms. Justice will sound bells and screams to alert you to the fact that something is not right. Your gut instincts will be strong and you will know to investigate. The actuality of the deception may not be readily apparent, but the fact that it is there will be obvious. Now, you know to investigate. Now you know to look for the truth so that you have what you need to call out the dishonest ones and set right what is wrong.

The Justice piece of you has the ability to see past deception to ascertain the truth behind the lies. It is able to see through the mask that somebody wears into the real person behind it. What does this person look like? What is their real nature? Why do they hide this aspect of their self? Is it to hide a lie, or are they protecting their self out of fear? Fear of what? Fear that their real true self is inadequate? Fear that they will not be accepted, respected or liked? The Justice piece of you sees right through it. If it is applicable to do so, you put them at ease and let them know they are accepted. If though, you discover the mask hides a trail of untruths, you may call them out on them. Make them face their deception and answer for it. The ability to fairly assess a situation to determine all the factors involved so that a sound determination can be made is a hallmark of Justice.

To keep your power of assessment in check and not be overbearing when dealing with other people is another hallmark of Justice. You remain grounded and balanced in dealing with others as not to be overly judgmental. Likewise, you are not too quick to render a verdict in a conflict, but are willing to hear all sides of a story to establish fairness. You are capable of removing your ego when assessing a situation so that the final rendering is about those involved and not you. You remain a disinterested third party in the name of balance and integrity.

The Justice piece of you is acutely aware of the consequences of all actions. In a perfect setting, good deeds will result in good things. Bad deeds will result in bad things. But a blurry line may separate the two. When deliberately acting to deceive, it is easy to imagine that karma will come back to you and teach you a lesson about that kind of thing later. Doing good for the sake of creating a positive end result can bring to mind a rewarding return of a karmic investment. What happens though when you must do something seemingly negative for the sake a greater good to come? What if you must sacrifice one friend for the sake of another? In a case such as that, it is your intention that matters, because let's face reality. Being perfectly fair is not always possible. If you know that what you are doing is what you need to do, and the final result has some amount of good to it, there is no reason to beat yourself up. Offer apologies where needed and know you did the right thing. Then move on.

Redemption is a yearning that your inner Justice piece cries out for. It likes it when wrongs are made right and it is not blamed for something it never had any business being blamed for in the first place. When an unjust prosecution is reversed, the Justice piece of you sings with joy. It breathes a sigh of relief and is glad for the unjustly accused party that is has been released of its harsh judgment and has had its reputation restored.

The Justice piece of you doesn't ask for much, but what it does ask for, it demands. All it really wants is fairness. It wants truth, and it wants what's right. Honor this piece of yourself and you will remain rightfully balanced.

THE HANGED MAN

Do this. Stand on your head. Or, at the very least lay down with your head lower than your feet and look at your environment from this perspective. Now, the ceiling is the floor and the floor is coming at you from a whole other direction. It's the same room, right? Suddenly it looks completely different, that's all. As you look at the room from this other angle, you're seeing things you haven't seen in it before. This is your inner Hanged Man's way of seeing the world. From the Hanged Man's perspective, there is no reason to stay stuck in a single mindset. There is no reason to see things from one angle. There is no one perfect answer to any question or problem. When searching for an answer or a solution, your Inner Hanged Man will examine all the angles, even the least obvious one. Somewhere unexpected, the best answer waits to be discovered.

How can you find solutions to your problems from the same angle from which you plunged into them? Generally speaking, you cannot. The best fixes are found by looking at the situation from a different perspective to create a different mindset. What is your brain telling you about the situation? Is your brain keeping you trapped in a situation you do not like just because it can't find an escape from it? Is it insistent that this is just how it is, so you will just have to live with it? Your inner Hanged Man knows better, and will never listen to such a simplistic notion.

He will immediately examine the situation. He will look at it up close, zoomed out, upside down, inside out, right side up, in the light, and in the dark. He will smell it, touch it, taste it, listen to it, and ask it questions. He will keep searching for clues and solutions after others give up. To your inner Hanged Man, challenges problems, and difficulties are nothing more than opportunities to shine, because they give him the opportunity to demonstrate his power.

Looking at situations from other perspectives, do you not see what important details that you did not see before? Consider these new details. They are vitally important to understanding the whole of the situation. With these new facts in the light, does the picture not seem different? Does the situation now seem to be completely different? The situation has not changed, but your understanding of it has.

Remember, nothing is flatly two dimensional. Every situation has many angles and many facets. Consider them all. Once you do this, you will understand how to escape those that cause distress. To escape means to remove yourself from the situation, as well as gaining an understanding of how you got there to begin with.

A variety of understandings will come to you as you examine all the angles of a situation. One of those understandings may very well be that things are as they are and that is how they are meant to be so why try to change it? That is a real possibility. But how will you know that if you don't thoroughly examine the situation to see that for yourself? So if you don't find the solution you were hoping to find, don't feel bad about it. There just wasn't a solution there. It is meant to be as it is and there is nothing you can do about it.

If there is nothing you can do about it, why worry about it? Why spend your energy whining and complaining about things that you cannot control? Maybe it's raining. Maybe you don't want it to rain. Can you do anything to stop the rain? No. You can't. So quit complaining about the rain! All you can do is get into the flow of the rain. Adjust yourself to it. Carry an umbrella. Wear a raincoat. Put some boots on. Whatever. The rain isn't going to stop just to suit your wants and needs. Get that through your head. What in your life represents this rain? What can you not change that you wish you could, but can't? Adjust yourself to it and be happy no matter what.

You can't be in control of everything, and why would you want to be? If you were in control of everything, where would the surprises come from?

Where would the issues arrive from that allow you to develop the strength to deal with them? When would your problem solving skills ever come into play? How would you ever grow? How would you ever evolve? You need a little opposition in your life in order to propel you to become the person you need to be. So accept when you can't be in charge of all aspects of what's going on in your life. Say, "It is what it is" when what it is is without your ability to change it.

Your inner Hanged Man gives you perspective. He gives you facts, and facts equal freedom. Your inner Hanged Man takes into consideration the other frames of reference of a situation so you can see it from a larger perspective.

DEATH

There is a piece of you that is ready to face the inevitability of change. Sometimes it fears this change. Other times, it does not. It may even be waiting for it, willing it to come. The anticipation of this change can be exciting, or it can be stressful. It may even create a sensation of ambivalence, because whatever this change that is coming is not really that exciting. Unless it is. You may not know until you experience it. This piece of you is Death, and it knows nothing can stay the same.

Death is about the defining moments in life when the paradigm shifts and there is no going back. Dying can hurt like hell, but for the prospect of new life, it is worth the agony. So don't let things get to you. Take a "What doesn't kill you makes you stronger" approach to living. To find strength in change is to appreciate the journey that has brought you to where you are, so open your eyes to the milestones that mark the changes that characterize the significant moments of your life.

To die is to be liberated, released from an unpleasant situation and feel the burden of it lifted from you. Say "Enough is enough." Bring an end to a circumstance that isn't working out for you. Be honest with yourself about how things are going. Be far-seeing and predict how the present will slip into the future and what the impact will be. If it doesn't look good to you, start over with a new beginning. Start from scratch. Create a rebirth that looks like it will grow into the life you would like to live.

New chapters can begin when sudden changes are thrust upon you. In this case, be able to go with the flow. Adapt. Adjust. Get used to the changes. New chapters can also begin with Ah-Ha! moments. You think you have everything figured out, then all of a sudden something completely throws you off into a new mindset. This could be something that brings feelings of happiness, or it could be the realization of of something quite sad for you. It could be an answer to a grand question that has been perplexing you. Suddenly, the answer is there! This changes everything. Accept that change is a part of life. Acclimate yourself to these changes when they come.

Write a new chapter of your life on your own accord before somebody else writes it for you. Assess for yourself what is working and what is not, what still fits and what doesn't, and what should stay the same and what should change. Then come up with and implement a plan to create these changes before these changes get forced on you. Take control of your own destiny. You will be a lot happier with what comes your way when you do.

Giving control over your life to others puts you in the passenger seat. What are you doing in the passenger seat of your own life? This is your life! Get in the driver's seat and take control! If you don't, you are going to end up where it is most convenient for somebody else. You have a much better idea of where you want to be and the best route to get there. Ask for advice when you need it, of course. Consider what others have to say, but make your own decisions. Steer your own life, and blaze your own path. Choose your own adventures and write your own endings. New chapters begin when we reach goals. So set goals. Reach them. Change your life as you begin a new chapter.

You have to wrap up things from the past before you can successfully move forward. Old objects hold old energy. This energy can keep you stuck in a time best moved on from. Clean the physical clutter of your life. Don't cling to physical objects. Appreciate them in the moment. Appreciate them for a time, then let go. Release. Clear. Make room for the path ahead. Don't be held back by the emotions and the energy, these objects bind you to. Let go. Be light. Even as you blaze your own unique path, you do not want to trip over the emotional debris of the past. It will show up unexpectedly beneath your feet unless you step back and clear it up.

The piece of you that is Death has a great appreciation for life. It loves life so much that it wants to see it optimized. For it to be optimized, it must change. It must evolve. The Death within you knows that change and evolution can only happen if you die, and then become reborn.

TEMPERANCE

Temperance brings to mind alchemy. Imagine the bringing together of elements and of energies to create a unified whole. Once blended, something new is created. We no longer have a bit of this and a bit of that. No, what we have now is an entirely new entity made up of all these individual elements. The Temperance piece of you feels this energy. It senses the different components as they come together and is aware of the blending of the new whole.

None of us live in a vacuum. We are receptive of the energies that others put out, just as they are receptive of the energy that we ourselves put out. Take a look at how your actions, reactions, attitude and general disposition effect a situation and the people around you. Do you promote harmony or disharmony? Or are you completely neutral? How do you feel in the crowd? How do you feel in various situations? Are you comfortable or uncomfortable? What is it about the situation that makes you feel this way? Can you pinpoint it? We can't always control how others will feel around us. The best we can do sometimes is to try not to put out too much negative energy, and endeavor as we can to not be a downer that is going to make others feel drained.

Sometimes, do you ever just feel weird, or a little off but you are not sure why? Do you ever wonder where certain feelings you are feeling are coming from and what they have to do with you? Does this happen in a crowd or around certain individuals? In certain places? Those of an empathetic nature are particularly prone to this phenomenon. When this happens, it is time for some Temperance deconstruction. Examine the situation you are in and the people around you. What can you tell about these people just by observing their actions, attitudes, body language, and general demeanor? Are they happy people? Upset? Angry? Something else? As you identify their demeanor, how do you feel? Would you say that you yourself feel what you have identified in them? Is there a logical reason for you to feel this way? Maybe you have absorbed what they are putting out.

Visualize a car engine. Imagine an apprentice mechanic curious to know how this car engine works, so he takes on the task of taking it apart, bit by bit and piece by piece. In so doing, he is learning what all the pieces are and where they go, and possibly even what they do. Apply this to your life. Be curious about your energetic construction. Start taking it apart. Consider each energetic building block. What does each contribute to the whole of who you are? Which ones are positive, which ones are negative, and which don't make sense to you at all?

Temperance is to understand and appreciate the needs and interests of the people we encounter and to adjust our energy level towards them as to not overwhelm them. This is a basic consideration of the people you encounter, and we can hope for this courtesy to be shown to us.

Imagine their energy as a wave coming at you. Imagine yourself as a sponge unwittingly absorbing these waves. Now they are clinging to you. You are stuck with them. But they are not organic to you, so why do you want them? Know for yourself that you should be feeling good and content, but this foreign energy is twisting your senses into something that makes no sense to you. Peel away anything that does not support feeling good and be done with it. Wring this proverbial sponge of all energy that is not your contentment. This is to deconstruct the energetic makeup of you. It is a healthy and wise practice.

THE DEVIL

The Devil exists inside of you as a piece of who you are. He is not an external force acting on you. He is those feelings of inferiority that keep you down. He is those feelings of doubt and guilt that have no foundation. He is that voice in your head that tells you, oh so convincingly, that you are not good enough, that people don't like you, that you are stupid, and that nothing you do is right. He is there to block your path when you try to move forward. He is that cloud when you want to bask in the sun. He is the potholes in the road of your personal journey. To live fully, you must defeat him. You must get past him. You must accept him for what he is and not subjugate yourself to his whims. You must not give in to the illusion of pain he throws your way. Teach yourself to not hear his destructive voices and to accept that what he throws in front of you to stop you from succeeding is nothing but illusions to keep you in pain.

Most of us do not live in pain. We live in the memory of pain. This memory of pain instigates a fear of pain. These are our shadows. These are our triggers. These are our buttons that get pushed. This is the piece of us that is The Devil, and the demons we face. Fear is a pushback to happiness that keeps us from experiencing life to the fullest. What is fear but an anticipation of an attack? Sometimes these fears are rational, while many other times they are not. A phobia, such as a fear of talking to people, which will only slow you down in the realm of social advancement, is not rational. The fear of bears or the fear of sharks may very well keep you alive; these are rational. The fear of pain is The Devil's way of keeping us trapped in a fog.

Your inner Devil can distort your perception of reality and convince you that people mean you harm. Do these people know this though? This is a drama playing out in your head, with The Devil as the director calling the shots. These people who are supposedly out to get you are just going through the motions of their own life. They are not focused you. They mean you no harm. They have no idea of the pain you were once in and that they are reminding you of it. Yet, you are reacting to them as if you expect the worse from them. This will put an edge on your energy that they will feel and react to. They will wonder why you are as you are.

The memory of emotional pain can be a powerful influence. It is easy to expect more. When you find yourself in a similar situation that you were in just before the pain came to you in the past, the memory of the pain causes you to brace for the pain once again. This can be irrational yet at the same time completely understandable as the memory of this pain can cause distress to the point you are convinced that the pain is going to surface again. You are sure that the anticipation of the pain is warranted in some way. You are certain that the pain is about to happen and it causes stress.

The thing to do is imagine the pain to be a storm cloud, and your true place in relation to it is above it, so imagine that you are rising above. Find yourself on the other side of it, above it where you have the proper perspective on it. It is beneath you. It cannot hurt you from down there. Below the clouds it is dark. Above the clouds, it is light. Stay above.
You must remember, the memory of pain is not the same as actual pain. You have grown from the person who first felt that pain. The person who first felt that pain may not even exist anymore. You may have changed so much that the paradigm in which that pain existed does not even exist anymore. You must remind yourself of this.

When you feel the triggers of an old pain beginning to happen, examine who you are in relation to who you used to be. Keep yourself on this elevated level. Remind yourself that you are a new person now. The lesson that this old pain was designed to teach you has been learned. Remind yourself of this. If you have learned it already, why do you need to go through it again? You don't. Therefore it cannot be real. Therefore, it is imagined. It is all in your head. This is a memory that exists only in your mind. It can only be as painful as you allow it to be. Dismiss this memory. Put it behind you. With nothing to attach to, it will simply go away. In this way, you beat the Devil- your personal Devil.

THE TOWER

Humankind is not meant to stagnate. Humankind is meant to grow, to change and evolve. We are meant to constantly innovate and continuously create. This is a species wide mandate as well as a personal mission. None of us alive on the earth are meant to stay exactly the same through all the years of our lives. Just as our bodies change as we grow older, so do our ideas and our attitudes. These new ideas and attitudes guide us towards the purpose of our life.

The trick to evolution is to be open to these new ideas and attitudes. Sometimes we get so stuck in our ideas that we, without hesitation, resist anything new that occurs to us. When we feel resistance to our new notions, it is advisable to revolt against the resistance in the name of revolution. Revolt against rigid thinking! Rebel against stuck thoughts! This revolutionary rebel piece of you is The Tower. Let it guide your meditation towards this overthrow of limited viewpoints. See your new ideas in a box atop a tower, stuck and imprisoned, unable to see the light of day. Now, see a lightning bolt striking this box, liberating them as the thought forms that guarded them fall away.

The power of your inner Tower is your ability to watch it all fall, to bid it all farewell without a tear in your eye. Knock down your towers. Set your soul free. So much trapped energy is in a tower. Nothing is flowing. Nothing is moving. It's just stuck. Just stagnant. This is destructive. This is overpowering. It is invasive to common sense. Knock the Tower down. Set that energy to the wind. Watch it blow away. Feel yourself become lighter without the weight of stuck energy bearing down on your shoulders. Do this by examining your life truly. Don't kid yourself. Don't lie to yourself. Honestly access what thoughts, attitudes, and beliefs are not serving you. Once you have them, let them go. Just, simply, stop clinging to them. Say goodbye and watch them waft away. You have to be honest with yourself; that is the most important and probably the most difficult part of the process. If you can manage to do it though, wow! Life gets good. So give it a try.

This is the long awaited revolution. This is a personal thing, a personal revolution. This is to take stock of your own limiting beliefs and agents of procrastination. This is to take note of those voices that are telling you why something cannot or should not be done, or why everything is just fine the way it is without any need to change, encouraging you to be complacent even though in your heart you are fully aware that things are missing, that something about this paradigm is unsatisfactory and just not right. You know this. You feel this. You sense that there can be more, that life can be more fulfilling. Your heart knows there needs to be change, even when your head says otherwise.

When you wake up to your purpose, not just partially but fully, you ignite a fire. To live fully is to be on fire- to have your sparks of desire become a fire, a flame, an inferno. For this to happen, you must eliminate all that is convincing you that you cannot. You must have the attitude of a warrior. You must instigate an internal revolution. You must face these agents of negativity head on and eliminate them. They have been in control for too long. They have been telling you false facts long enough.

These false facts are that what you are trying to accomplish is not doable, that your lot in life is set. They are telling you that you will always be this, that, or whatever you are. But your heart knows you can be more. Or it may tell you can always do it tomorrow- that it will take care of itself tomorrow, tomorrow, tomorrow. Don't think about it today, let tomorrow handle it. Tomorrow comes, tomorrow comes, tomorrow comes, and nothing happened. Realize this- tomorrow doesn't care. When you put something off until tomorrow, you put your destiny and your purpose in the hands of an empty and uncaring entity.

You know what you want. You do. Your heart has been telling you for ages. But there's your mind convincing you that you can't have it, or that it will "just happen." The mind is not always one with the spirit. You must get past this. This is the spirit's revolution, to get past the mind's reasoning as to why something can't be done, or that it can be done later. The spirit is meant to fly, so don't let the mind cage it. The spirit must revolt and break free of the cage that the mind puts it in. This is the revolution that will lead to evolution, for when we are following our spirit's desire, we accomplish the missions of our life and we live fully. By accomplishing our missions, we evolve. The more we do it as individuals, the easier it is to do it as a species. That's how simple it is. Use your inner Tower to remind you of this.

THE STAR

The piece of you that is The Star is that which you feel appreciated for, and remember, the sun is a star. The sun is what makes people feel good. The sun creates a gravitational pull that others orbit around. So when you are shining as a Star, others will bask in your light. Your light is your talents and your skills. Your light is what makes you uniquely you. Your light is what inspires others. So, shine brightly and inspire greatly.

To own your Star power is to know and understand your talents and your strengths, and to utilize them to their maximum potential, so much so that nay-sayers and critics cannot offend or bother you. You draw into yourself all you need to be truly great and shine as brightly as you are capable of shining no matter what dark clouds are present. People appreciate your charismatic nature. You have put in the work to develop your skills and talents and you are able to do perfectly what others struggle with, being uninhibited within the context of your power and your talents.

Appreciate the fact that people appreciate you. Instead of shutting somebody down when they tell you something good about yourself, say "Thank you." Or, "Thank you, I appreciate that." It doesn't mean you have a big head just because you are aware of your talents. Open yourself to appreciation. You know what you are good at so why not accept the accolades that come your way for it?

Take compliments. Don't feel like you have to be humble when somebody says something about how much they appreciate you or something that you have accomplished. You have skills and talents. These are what make you shine. These are what set you apart from other people. These are a part of the reason people are drawn to you. This is your Star. This is what makes you stand out. Why would you fight that?

It is so easy to reject a compliment. It is so easy to think we have to be humble all the time so that when somebody says something nice to us, we automatically say "No, no. I don't deserve that. It's nothing." Why though? Why do we do that? Why do we not let others appreciate us? Don't we appreciate others? Of course we do, so let them appreciate you as well.

Once we know that people in our life support and appreciate us, what we are able to do, then we are more comfortable with it. Now we feel like we have permission to shine. Try to not wait for this permission. Identify within yourself these shining lights of Star power and shine them as brightly as possible no matter what fear you have of what others may think or of what jealousies they may inspire.

You can't control what people think of you or how they will respond to your attempts to do great things, or how they will respond to how great the things are that you do. You can't control how people will react to other people's reactions to your greatness either. So why worry about it? Continue to aim high and aspire to awesomeness, and let the chips fall where they may. Let the nay-sayers say nay; it doesn't mean you have to respond. Keep doing what you do until they realize their nay-saying is falling on deaf ears. Then hopefully they will shut up and let you do your thing unbothered.

The thing to do is, do your thing, do it greatly, and feel good about it. Don't feel bad about the things you can't do, even if you wish you could do them. Let those that are good at those things have the glory for it. Remember, not everybody is meant to be a nuclear-astro-physicist. Not everybody needs to be. So let the nuclear-astro-physicists of the world take care of all that kind of stuff. Not everybody needs to be a brilliant guitar player. So let the brilliant guitar players have their day. Same goes for the brilliant novelists, poets, doctors, marathon runners, and all the other people that are great at whatever they are great at. Appreciate them, but focus on what you are great at so that they can appreciate you back.

Your inner Star offers validation that you are awesome in the ways that make you shine. Don't be inhibited. In your mind's eye, create your own private elevator that will take you directly to the top. Make it a luxurious express elevator that doesn't stop until it reaches the top, and you don't need to explain yourself to anybody for being on it. Now imagine what it looks like at the top. What is the view? What gifts do you find waiting for you up there? What are your special powers when you are at the top? These special powers are the pieces of you that are your Star.

THE MOON

Feel like you are going mad? Maybe a little crazy? Lost? Confused? Uncertain? It's not your imagination. You really are. But don't worry about it. It's just The Moon asserting it's power over you. It won't last forever. It's just the Moon doing what it does.

The piece of you that is The Moon is like that. It throws uncertainty into the mix to make you doubt yourself and wonder whether or not you're completely sane. Completely sane would be a lot to ask when the Moon is acting on us. It really does make us lose a little of our sanity. Just accept it and make the necessary accommodations. When you don't quite feel like your self, try not to make major decisions. When you feel threats to your sanity, really think through what you are contemplating doing. Don't do something you will regret just because you didn't take the time for a clearer head to prevail.

Our inner Moon creates mystery. It's that piece of who we are that makes us ask, "What exactly is going on? Why do I feel weird? What am I forgetting? Where am I? What should I be doing? How is everything going to work out? Does anybody care? Am I all alone? Does anybody love me?" The uncertainty of the Moon can create paranoia. Hold strong in these moments. Ride it out. The moon, in its cyclical nature, will eventually swing back around to a more rational position for you and you will understand yourself, the things, and the people around you again.

Sometimes you don't know something. No matter how much it drives you crazy not to know it, you have to accept that you don't. Your mind will go to work filling in the blanks of what you don't know, and most likely this will go to some extreme that is not authentic. It may assume the worst of a situation. But what does your brain know about it? That's the problem. It doesn't know all the facts, so it creates fictions. Based on what it thinks it knows, it fills in the gaps with whatever it can come up with. After it comes up with one scenario, it will probably stop. It won't keep going and create alternative scenarios that perhaps have a more positive outcome. Then you sit with that scenario, convinced that it is real. Then you get upset because you don't like it. Then you react to this outcome as if it has already come to pass. And this reaction is irrational. It is best to wait for the Moon energy to pass before reacting to anything. Otherwise, you run the risk of getting upset over things that don't matter, or don't even exist at all.

You inner Moon urges you to have patience and let things play out as they naturally will without trying to have an influence over it. Show respect for the natural flow of things. Things are happening as they are meant to. Wishing they will go this way or go that way will not send them in this direction or that direction. Anticipate which direction they will go and let your intuition guide you from there. Anticipate how things will work out for you in all case scenarios. If the natural flow of the situation goes in one direction, how is that for you? If it flows in the other direction, how is that for you? What other direction might it flow? When you anticipate the different directions the flow may go, you can prepare yourself for the different eventualities.

Let your intuition lead you. Be comfortable within the mystery without absolutely needing exact answers and exact coordinates. Understand that not everything will make sense right off, but that you may need to fumble about some as you figure things out. Be okay with that. Be willing to learn as you go. Have faith that clarity will present itself if you have patience. This is as the Moon cycles, and you can't just shut your inner Moon off when it gets weird or uncomfortable, so you might as well learn to ride out its cycles.

THE SUN

"If you're not having fun, then you're doing it wrong." The piece of you that is the Sun is giving you that advice. Listen to it. It's a good motto to live by. Why focus on things that make you miserable when you can focus on the things that make you happy? Forget stress. Forget pressure. Forget regrets, grudges, anger, all that. Focus on enjoying life. What does it take to do that? How can you facilitate your own joy? Is it a trip to the beach? Well then, make sure you get to the beach soon. Does it mean watching a movie with somebody you like to watch movies with? Then make a plan to watch a movie with that person. Does it take a long drive in the country? Then get in your car and go. Find your sun. Find what makes you feel good. Find it and soak it in. Find time for it.

If there is anything that keeps your inner Sun from shining as brightly as it can, it would be the imposition of negativity. Holding onto darkness and bad feelings will prevent the light that you have every right to feel from reaching you. What's the point of doing that? Take an honest inventory of what you are holding onto. Take note of what is overshadowing you and keeping you from feeling as good as you can about yourself. If feeling good about yourself means finding the fortitude to forgive somebody for something or other, then do it. Find the fortitude. Whatever you have against them, let it go. If they make you angry, get past it. Maintain a positive disposition and do not let anybody's negativity eat at you. Free yourself of the darkness of negativity and bask in the light of forgiveness.

Examine who brings out your best qualities and brightens your life, and who makes you feel good. Give these people your focus and your energy, for they are deserving. Notice who drains your energy and brings out your worst qualities. Avoid these people as best you can, for they serve no benefit to you. None.

To have a good day is to allow yourself to have a good day. Simple as that. You may be tempted to let little things bother you: your neighbor's barking dog, too much traffic on your daily commute, rude people at the grocery store. But don't. Don't let these things get to you. Rise above and see beyond them. Your life is richer and fuller than anything these petty nuisances can deteriorate. Let life make you feel good. Appreciate the air you breathe and the food you eat. Let this day be a day to appreciate all that the earth has to offer. Appreciate warmth. Appreciate companionship. Appreciate talents. Appreciate alone time. Enjoy the your inner Sun and appreciate living.

To have a good day, or to have a bad day, it's really all a mindset. It may be cloudy, rainy or colder than you like, so you tell yourself it is going to be a bad day. But does it have to be just because you told yourself it will be? It's all in your perception. Whatever the conditions of the day, whatever the weather, you can still find the good in it. So don't settle for bad days. Find what there is to appreciate about the moments of your life, then appreciate them. What you find may be as small as the feel of the breeze across your face or a favorite song that you haven't heard in a while. Whatever you find, enjoy it.

There is always something to enjoy. It may be as small as the feel of the breeze across your face or a favorite song that you haven't heard in a while. So, no matter what your circumstances are in any given moment, find something to feel good about. Don't root yourself too firmly in unhappiness. Allow whatever small thing that might lift you out of it to do so. Why put up with feeling bad? You don't have to. Be open to happiness. You have that piece of you that is The Sun to help you with that. Use it. Don't dwell on the negative. If you do, you will just find more and more negativity. Dwell instead on the positive. Isn't finding more and more positive better? Even if your day isn't taking shape the way you had hoped it would, let the piece of you that is the Sun remind you to enjoy it no matter what.

JUDGMENT

Judgment is a harsh word. It brings to mind retribution and punishment. It makes it seem like you've done something wrong and are waiting for a verdict that is going to determine your fate based on somebody's or some entity's infallible ruling. That can be scary, especially if you have a guilty conscious. Assessment is a nicer idea. It's also more accurate.

This assessment is not of all that you have done wrong or right, but what the balance is between what you could have done and what you actually did do. Did you take the highroad or the lowroad in moments of decision? Did you enlighten others or diminish them? Did you make the choices that contributed to your own highest good, even when it was not the easiest or most fun thing to do, or did you make a habit of taking the easy way out? Did you tell the truth when it would have been easier to tell a lie?

Every day, choices have been presented to you. How have the ones you made added up? They have all led up to who you are right now, in this very minute. What do you think? Happy with everything? Wish you had done something differently? How would have doing things differently in the past changed this moment for you right now? Will this impact the next decision you make as you speculate where it may lead based on what you have decided in the past?

Don't think of judgment or assessment as if some divine forces are watching your every move, shaking their head in distain every time you make a decision they don't like, because that's not what's going on. These divine entities are not going to smack you down if you do something that displeases them. So don't worry if you go five miles over the speed limit or reach across the table to grab the salt instead of asking somebody to pass it to you. You are not going to be subjected to any harsh criticism from the divine realm over these things. A ticket and a heavy sigh from somebody who is tired of what they themselves consider rude behavior from you on the earthly plane is likely all you will get. Decide for yourself what that means to you and how you want to adjust your future actions based on it.

The piece of you that is Judgment is the piece that knows your true capabilities, even those that have lain in latency for years. It knows your truest and highest potential, and it knows where you are in relation to achieving it. It knows what you are on the earth to do and when you are meant to wake up to it. This is the piece that will shake you awake and smack you to get your attention, saying, "Hey! You know what to do! Why aren't you doing it?" when you get too far off course. This is the piece of you that assesses your actions and the decisions you have made as they relate to your highest purpose, and nudge you towards the track that will take you there. It doesn't judge you though. It holds nothing against you if you are not in perfect alignment with your life's purpose. Its only purpose is to guide you. It wants you to live up to your highest potential, and will do its part to get you there.

Judgment is the ability to fairly and accurately assess a situation and understand where everything stands within it, what is working, and what is not. It is the ability to appreciate and understand what needs to happen next, and to truly know if you are ready to say that a goal has been reached or that a situation is complete before declaring it done. It is the ability to see all the details and see what is missing, what works, and what needs to be augmented. Think of it in terms of writing a book. You got all the words down, but are they spelled correctly? Are the commas and semicolons and all that being used correctly? Is it exactly as it should be? Are you happy with it, or does it need another revision? Apply that principle to everything that is important to you. Ask yourself, "Is it as perfect as it can be?" If you feel it is, then it is done.

Have you been feeling like you have been spinning your wheels? Working, trying, hoping, trying, hoping, working, but you just don't seem to be getting anything done or getting anywhere? Well then, stop for a minute. Just stop. Stop trying. Stop fretting. Stop worrying. Stop everything. Stop everything and examine what all this effort has been about. This that you are trying to achieve, is this even the best flow for you to be in? Is this even something that you need to worry about? Is this actually important in the grand scheme of your life? It might not be. Upon examination, you may realize that none of it matters anyway. You may realize that this isn't congruent with the life you should be living. In that case, move on from it. Realize and accept the unimportance of it and find something to focus on that is more in the flow of your life. Accept this as your wake up call. It is time to let go.

Sometimes, step out of yourself and assess yourself as an outsider. What do you see to be your weaknesses? Your flaws? Your strengths? Your talents? Your star qualities? Your dimness? Your light? How have the decisions you made created the person you are? What, can you imagine, might you have done differently to create a different outcome? What can you do now to course correct and compensate for what you are unhappy with? How can you do more of the things that please you?

The piece of you that is Judgment will assess how far you have traveled on the path of your life's journey, and question if you have learned and integrated the lessons that have been presented to you that take you to your perfection. Are you past the same repeating patterns that keep you stuck in the same place? Have you amassed the wisdom necessary to take you to the next plateau of life? If yes, you may proceed. If not, you must go back and repeat the learning opportunities that your choices denied you. The sooner you learn and integrate these lessons, the sooner you can move on. How do you know what these lessons are that you need to get past? You figure them out by examining the patterns of your life. What is it that you get stuck on and say, "Here I go again. Why does this always happen to me?" These are clues. To consciously try to get beyond these things gets you past these things. Once lessons are learned and integrated, you can move onto new and other aspects of your perfection.

THE WORLD

To arrive at The World means you have successfully met the challenges that life has thrown at you on your way to a grand and purposeful objective. Although these challenges were numerous, and they often seemed insurmountable, you dug deep, you persevered, you stuck with it to get past them to achieve your goals and your purpose. This is not a small accomplishment. Not everybody has what it takes to get past the obstacles and hurdles to achieve this. It takes courage to get through the dark times. It takes fortitude to not give up when the going gets rough. It takes a certain brilliance to see the light at the end the tunnel. The World is an exclusive destination that the fearful seldom reach.

Many people, while comfortable in the light, are fearful of the dark. In the light, we see what is in front of us. We have greater sense of what we are getting ourselves into. We see what is coming our way and we can joyfully anticipate what to expect from it. While there is much light on our journey to The World, it is easy to focus on the dark. The dark brings us pain. The dark instigates uneasy anticipation. We put up our guard against this, and this takes energy which can ultimately sap us energy and make us feel emotionally and physically drained. Who wants this? What good does it do us to feel such pain?

The good that this pain does is in that it forces our focus. When we are in pain, we focus on the feeling of the pain, and how we wish it wasn't there.

We focus on the cause of the pain and wish we could do something about it. This focusing, if properly directed, can turn to mindfulness. Instead of treating the pain and its source as something horrific that we must endure, turn it around and see it as a clue to what we need to be truly whole and truly healed. Pain is something that is unresolved. What will it take to resolve it? Forgiveness? Communication? Meditation or hypnotherapy to see into the pain what is not on the surface and obvious?

Imagine that all the unresolved pain and sorrow from your life is still within you, taking physical form and space. Seriously look at these forms and identify them for what they are- unresolved issues, then deal with them in a constructive way. Each one represents a hope or an expectation that got dashed. You had hoped for a positive outcome, but a negative one came your way. You had expected normalcy, but instead things changed unexpectedly and against your will, and you never had a chance to adjust to the change; it was thrust onto you without you first having a chance to brace for it. Each of these could have had a different outcome in their original occurrence, one that did not create the pain that it did. Imagine now how it would feel if a more positive outcome had occurred. Imagine that it went that way. Imagine now, based on that alternative outcome, how your life would be different. Feel the ripples of change catch up to you. Let these ripples create the changes you would like to feel. The changes may only be in your mind, but by their power in your mind, they can dissolve the physical forms that the pain has created. The difference this makes is incredible.

The thing to do now is fill that space with pure white, healing light. Without the heaviness that was just there, you are not stuck on the ground, mired in the stagnant muck of sadness and pain. You are now free and light. You can now ascend and fly. So fly. Ask your spirit where it wants to go and let it lead the way. Don't tether your spirit to any more weighty concerns.

Don't let your mind dictate where your spirit will go. Set your spirit free, and it will fly towards enlightenment. You just need to let it. The sooner you face your past pain, sorrow, and trauma, the sooner your spirit can set sail. The sooner your spirit sets sail, the sooner you find your truth and enlightenment. Why let fear slow you down? It is easy to run from it and hide from it all, but when you do that, you don't receive the benefits of defeating them. So find the courage and the fortitude to face your fears, sorrows, pains and traumas. This way, you take control of your destiny. You are not subjugating yourself to darkness.

The piece of you that is The World has a strong sense of accomplishment. It always has the final goal in its sight, a flicker of light in the distance that you are headed towards. The World piece of you will keep you on course towards that light. There will be obstacles on your way to it, there will be moments of doubt, there will be those times when you will question the validity of your pursuit, but your inner World will whisper, talk, scream and shout at you to keep going.

The realization of a goal or a dream may not look or feel as you imagine it will when you first start off in pursuit of it. The journey towards this realization may create shifts and changes along the way that alters the original vision of the actualization of the goal. It is a good idea to set goals with a loose idea its actualization. Have a firm idea of what you want to achieve, but be flexible to incorporate changes and new information.

There may actually be a number of alterations to what you finally arrive at. Will you be disappointed if the final realization is not precisely what you first concocted in your mind? Don't be, for as you embark on the journey towards the goal, the goal itself will perfect itself beyond what you knew of it at the start. This is more than just achieving a goal, this is achieving perfection. You have it figured out. What was once mysterious is now common knowledge. What once perplexed you, you now fully comprehend. You achieved this by being flexible.

Those that achieve their goals listen to their inner World. Those that do not, filter out this inner voice. They do not reach their ultimate goal, or if they do, it has become a bastardized version of it that is weakened significantly. Just know, there is a specific and strong goal you have set out to reach, and to reach it brings enlightenment. So endeavor to stay on track. Don't let the hard times overshadow the good times, because even though the journey may be difficult, you will also find light, breezy and easy times mixed into it. Soak in the strength of these good times and tap into them when the going gets tough.

The power of The World is the confidence it offers. You don't reach The World on your journey without gathering the strength, courage, integrity, and personal power to be there. This is what the journey there is about. It is not about reaching your destination and accomplishing your goals for the sake of doing so in and of itself, but rather to also gain the strength, wisdom, knowledge, and power that the journey provides. So by the time you are there, you have it. You are strong. You are powerful. You are wise and you are knowledgeable. It is about both the journey and the destination.

Part Two: Swords

The pieces of ourselves related to our thoughts

ACE OF SWORDS

Your intellectual potential is great. You truly have a brilliant mind. You are a genius, and a thinker of profound thoughts. Your ability to see past any deception to what is actual and true is astounding. This incredible brain power is the Ace of Swords within you. It is characterized by a sharp mind, the ability to know exactly what to say in any circumstance, a quick wit, strong analytical ability, intelligence, and brilliant ideas that are like seeds planted in your consciousness that could easily grow into million dollar concepts. All you have to do is tap into all this power.

To fully utilize the Ace of Swords within yourself means to tap into the power of your intellect. It means to brush aside anything that is filtering your brilliance. To filter your brilliance is to deny yourself its full strength. It's unfortunate, but that happens to everybody. We end up doubting ourselves. Despite how perfect our ideas are, we let ourselves be convinced that we can't possibly be that smart, that these ideas can't possibly be worthwhile. We may ask ourselves, who am I to have such thoughts? We may listen to those around us who cause self-doubt. They may say such things as, "Seriously? You think that will work? You think that is a good idea?" And we believe them. We let these voices talk us out of believing in ourselves. Instead of nurturing that seed of brilliance and coaxing it to grow to its full potential, we trample it, disallowing any growth from it. To do this denies ourselves of our true power.

An idea suddenly pops into your head. So many ideas have been stored inside of you for countless years just waiting for you to reach a point where you are not so stuck in your head to see them. Now they are finally free to come to the surface and be recognized. Here's what can happen- ideas get trapped inside of you somewhere. They are held prisoner by a mind and an ego that are so sure that they have all the answers that they do not allow for anything else to be noticed. When this happens, so many ideas get shoved aside and go unnoticed and unappreciated. How can they compete with an ego that is so sure of itself? When the ego makes up its mind, it is very hard to get it to accept anything else. With determination though, the ego will finally relax and allow for other concepts to come to the forefront. When this happens, you are said to be "inspired."

To focus on your brilliance, you need to free your mind of all the extraneous stuff that gets stuck there. All that stuff- the limiting beliefs, the fears, the worries, the assumptions, and the negative ideas you have come to believe about yourself- you need to see past it all. They do nothing to serve your higher purpose. It does nothing to coax that seed of brilliance into a strong and mighty entity. All it does is keep you from coming into your true power. It's all just chaos, and who needs it?

A mind free of chaos is a mind that can see what is real and what is not. What is real are those thoughts and impulses that lead to positive visualizations of positive outcomes, and the actualization of them. What is not real are those thoughts and impulses that tell you, without any consideration to the contrary, that nothing you are considering is valid. These are the thoughts that will keep you stagnant. They will hold you back from your full potential.

Before jumping to the conclusion that you cannot achieve your dreams, or that your ideas are not worthwhile, be sure to consider them. See them from all angles. Weigh them in your mind. Is there any validity the idea that these ideas are not good? Before dismissing them outright, be sure to look them over and see how they can be improved, and what changes could be made to perfect them. Don't let a chaotic mind keep you from doing this. A great idea may need refinement. Don't let yourself be talked into believing they are worthless before they are perfected. Spend time with your ideas and shape them into what they were always meant to be.

Take time every day to de-clutter your mind. A clear mind is a free mind. Spend a few moments, or more, in silence every day. Let your thoughts evaporate and your worries and cares drift away. What is left? This is what is important. This is what is authentic to you. This is what deserves your focus. These are the true thoughts and ideas that will grow into perfect fruition if allowed to do so. Every day, find what is beyond the clutter, and you will find your brilliance and you will embody the clarity that the Ace of Swords represents.

TWO OF SWORDS

You have a decision to make, and you need to just make it. You need to stop procrastinating. You need to stop making excuses why you haven't made it yet. You need to just make it already. This is the Two of Swords piece of you. It is the piece of you that has weighed all sides of the issue, has considered the variables, and has thought it all through sufficiently. Now you just need to stop hesitating and make up your mind.

Once you make up your mind, you know you are going to do something, but you pause just a little bit longer before you do it. Why? Maybe because this is something you'd rather not have to do, but you have to do it anyway. Maybe you are just unsure of yourself. You need just a little more time to think and a little more time before getting started. At some point though, you have to just say "I am ready." Then you have to do it.

Procrastinating does nothing but keep you stuck in your own head over an issue. The longer you put off doing whatever it is that you are not doing, the more you direct your thoughts to it, worry about it, and stress yourself out over it. What's the point of all that? Just do it. Have faith in yourself and get it done. Once you do, you don't have to think about it anymore. Once you are not thinking about it anymore, you are free of it. A free mind is an open mind. So open your mind by bringing an end to your procrastination.

There are those times when you are trying to think something through when it can be annoying to have to listen to other people who expect you to take on the weight of whatever it is that is on their mind, whether it is something relevant to the situation, or something mundane and pointless. These are the times when you really want to say, "Talk to the hand."

These people are coming at you, running their mouths, expecting you to listen to what they have to say, expecting you to care. But do you want to listen, or would you rather be alone with your own thoughts and not listen to these blow-hards prattle on?

Do you really care what they are talking about, or is it just another story about what their granddaughter did or the details of their cousin's hysterectomy operation, or some other thing that you have no interest in? Is it a request? Are they asking you to do something they could just as easily do their self? Are they asking you what time it is, when they could look at the clock on the wall their self? In these moments, it is perfectly normal to want to put up a shield and block these people out to stay focused on your own thoughts. It is acceptable to use those two swords to block access to your heart and warn people to not come close. You need this time to yourself.

Of course, you need to be polite, or should at least try to be. There is no reason to start an argument or a fight over something petty. Be patient and listen to what they have to say. Make them feel valued. It isn't always appropriate to put your hand up and tell them to be quiet. You really can't say, "Would you just shut up!" to anybody, no matter how badly they need to be told. So what can you do if you don't want to listen to them anymore? The best you can do is tolerate them and then slip away. If possible, avoid them altogether when you have something on your mind. This will give you peace, and you are entitled to peace. Be mindful of this and do your best to suffer these talkative people graciously.

The Two of Swords is that piece of you that recognizes that sometimes you need time to yourself to focus on your own thoughts. It is the piece of you that needs to think things through and weigh all the factors of an issue. Once you have thought it all though, act on it. Don't make excuses not to. Don't procrastinate. Take action and get things done.

THREE OF SWORDS

Sometimes you have to crack your heart open to really know what's inside of it. Sometimes you have to break it to understand it. Sometimes you have to bore a hole through it to see what makes it tick. Hearts are funny that way. When you are happy and your heart is full of love, don't you have a way of taking it for granted? Until it's hurting you might forget it's there altogether. Pain has a unique way of focusing our attention. The Three of Swords is the piece of you that feels that pain.

It is how you handle your pain that determines what you get out of it. Do you look for the lesson the pain is teaching you, or do you simply react to it? If you find the lesson that the pain has to teach you, you will grow from it, heal it, and it will contribute to your ultimate enlightenment. If you simply react, that's all you'll ever do and will never move beyond the rudimentary sensations it provides.

When your heart is filled with joy, you bask in that joy and don't question it. You're just glad to feel good. When is the last time you become pro-active against feeling happy and feeling good? Have you ever said, "I'm happy! Something must be wrong. I better do something about it." Most of us don't. That is because this is how we want to feel. Happiness is a good thing, so we let it ride. It's when our heart is filled with pain that we react the most strongly, because we want to lose that pain. This is when we need to crack our heart open and examine what's going on in there and ask, "Where is this pain coming from?"

We, quite naturally, react to immediate pain as it happens with the assumption that this pain exists on the surface of who we are without considering the deeper reality of it. Let's take the simple example of a romantic break-up. Say, you have been enjoying what you considered to be a really great relationship with somebody you felt like you were in love with, and you thought they were in love with you too. But then they say to you, "I want to break up and not see you anymore." Sure, this will hurt. Sure, this will break your heart. Sure, you will wish you didn't have to go through this and feel this way, but what choice do you have? There it is. The pain is real. It hurts. Your heart is broken. But you know what else? If you can consider your heart, instead of being "broken," to be "cracked open," you can go in and explore what's in there. You can find the answer to "What is the pain of this upset really attached to?" Think it's just the pain of the immediate circumstance? Dig a little deeper. There is probably more to it than just that.

Here is one way to think about it. Think about your heart as a storehouse of every experience you have ever had and a memory bank of every emotion you have ever felt. Something long forgotten that is stored away in the recesses of your heart may creep to the surface wanting to be addressed. Something, the shock of this recent breakup maybe, triggered it. It has been flushed out from where it was hiding to just below the surface of your awareness where it may have been lingering as an acute botheration. You can ignore it and wait for it to go away on its own, but do understand- even if it does recede on its own, it will one day be back in full effect with all the pain that there ever was still with it. This is not productive. This does not let you move on from the pain. This only puts the pain on hold until next time.

When you feel the stabbing of swords piercing your heart, look inside to see exactly what they are jabbing into. Most of the emotional pain we experience is attached to some experience we had at some point in life that was never properly healed. To trace your current pain back to some semblance of the original wounding is invaluable towards healing the pain. So take advantage of the pain you are in by examining it.

Fresh pain can instigate the surfacing of many emotions and feelings. This is a good thing even when it feels like a bad thing. It's a good thing because once these things come to the surface you don't have to dig for them in order to deal with them. When they surface, jump at the chance to examine them and address them and send healing energy to them. The pain of heartbreak, as it triggers old memories and old pain, gives you the chance to revisit the original occurrence of the pain so you can send it healing energy and take care of it once and for all.

You may be asking, "How do I do that? How do I send healing energy to the original occurrence of my pain if I don't know what that original occurrence is?" The answer is simple. Conjure an image of your inner child. Imagine your inner chid as vulnerable and needing protection. Consider the pain that you are in as a monster about to attack your inner child. Now step in and prevent that from happening. Shield your inner child from this monster and protect it. Don't let the pain monster carry out its assault. See your inner child protected and happy. See the smile it has on its face and feel the innocence and happiness it possesses. Appreciate the appreciation it has for you for saving it from the pain coming its way. Let this ripple through time and space, catching up to you as you are today.

When you feel the pangs of heartbreak, when you feel swords stabbing into you causing you anguish, don't let the opportunity to use it go to waste. Use it to crack your heart open and see what's there and heal it.

FOUR OF SWORDS

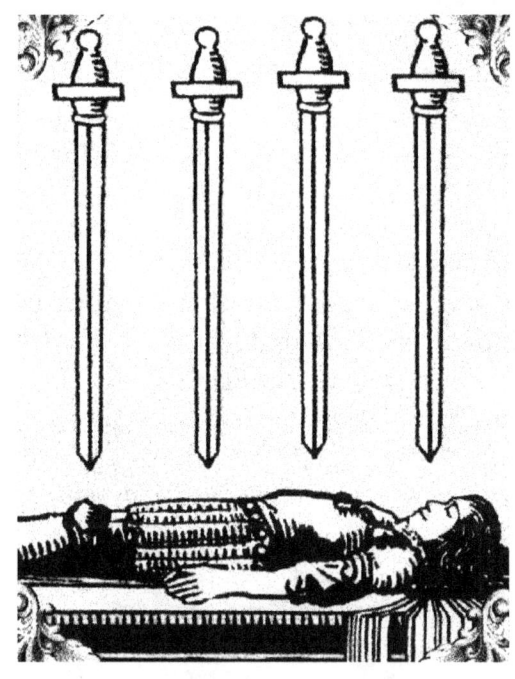

To go from chaos to calm can be a challenge. If you intend to stay healthy, sane, and happy, though you are going to have to. So often, this chaos is all in your mind. Sure, in our physical world chaos happens. So much happens all at once- too many people, too many things, too many demands and too much activity. How do you rationally deal with it all? How do you set priorities and decide what is the most important? You do your best, that's all. You do what you can to deal with it- one thing at time- trying not to let the craziness overwhelm you. When the chaos is in your mind, so too do you need a strategy to deal with it. The Four of Swords is that piece of you that seeks this calm.

Your mind is like that. It will go into hyperdrive sometimes with this thought, and that thought, this idea, and that idea. These thoughts and ideas will all come at you at the same time, bombarding you until you are completely boggled by them all and left wondering what's valid and what's just extra filler taking up space in your mind. You get too many thoughts happening all at once and next thing you know, you have a tangled up wad of confusion in your brain. Now you don't know what is real, what is honest, what is true or what serves your actual highest and best good. You don't know what thought is related to another or where one begins and another ends.

Some of your thoughts are positive, and some are negative, but which is which and which are pertinent and valuable? These thoughts have created a chaotic mass of confusion. But this is not how it should be. You need for your mind to calm down so you can figure out what is what. If you can't figure out what is what, how do you know how to proceed with any actions based on your thoughts? You end up responding to chaos with chaos, and all that chaos does nothing but begat more chaos, and chaos begotten by chaos becomes an uber-chaos that can really wear you down.

Take time to calm your mind so you can sort through what is useful and productive and what is not. Untangle your thoughts so, instead of a tangled up mess, you can see and examine each one as a unique entity, unaffected by the others. Teach yourself to find the thoughts that are not productive and turn them around to something more useful. Catch a random thought and examine it for validity. If it is not valid to whatever situation is at hand or to your life in general, dismiss it. If it is valid, ask yourself if it really truly is valid, because it might not be. Sometimes a thought will trick you into thinking it is important when it is not. Sometimes a thought will outright right lie to you about its own importance and gloat as it tricks you into believing its importance. Be careful about that. Ask of these thoughts, "Do they support valid reasoning? Do they point to a positive outcome, solution or inspiration?"

Once you have a good idea of which thoughts are the valid ones and which ones are not, you can latch onto a valid one and trace it through the knotted up mass of thoughts. Extract it from the thought wad and set it aside where it won't get lost or mixed back in with the others. Once you do that, go back to the thought wad and get another. Keep doing that until you have gotten all the valid thoughts you reasonably can. Now you can examine them away from the influence of the others. This is valuable because those other thoughts will still want your attention. They will still want to assert their authority. They will go to battle to get you to acknowledge their importance. Don't let them do that. Dismiss them.

To master the Four Swords within you, find time for this practice when you find too much on your mind. Rest. Meditate. Go for a walk in nature. Swim in the ocean if it's nearby. Exercise. Workout. Do whatever works for you to tame your mind and get focused. By focusing on the valid thoughts, you will be wise, focused, and calm. You don't have to wait until your thoughts get out of control, either. By creating a daily meditation practice, your thoughts are much less likely to get jumbled up to begin with.

FIVE OF SWORDS

Have you ever been through a hurricane? How about just a really bad storm? You know how tense and nervous that can make you feel? The wind blowing, the rain pounding, the lightning and the thunder a little too close? This can put you on edge and make you feel jump and jittery. Doesn't it make you wish it would just hurry up and be over already so you can let your guard down to relax? Then it finally ends. The rain finally stops. The wind calms itself. The thunder and lightning have moved on. Now you can breathe a sigh of relief that it's over. The Five of Swords is like that. It is that calm after the storm. It's the piece of you that desires an end to conflict. Whatever the conflict is- a fight, an argument, a falling out, frustration or anger- whatever. It's over. You survived. The clouds are breaking apart and the sun is shining through again. You don't need to be braced for an attack anymore. You can let go of worries.

What was it all about, anyway? This conflict that has ended? Was it really that important? So often, we convince ourselves that we have to be right. We get so worked up over things that the idea that we might not be right about it causes us stress. We look at the people who oppose our viewpoint as our enemies. We become so self-important that we defend our opinions almost to the death. "How can they be right if I am right? If I am right, they must be wrong!" And we can't just let it go. So we go on the attack. This causes them to attack back, which forces us to put energy toward being defensive. On and on this goes, back and forth, getting increasingly bitter. So much stress comes from this attitude. So many mental storms. And for what? Just to be right over some arbitrary and meaningless point? Because that's usually all it is. What's the point of that? Examine just how important it is anyway. Unless acquiescing will literally cause death, do you really need to have things your own way every time?

Give yourself a break. Relax your mind. Whatever battles you have been putting yourself through lately are over. Let go of whatever has been troubling you. Whatever worry and stress you have been struggling with is behind you. Allow yourself to accept that. Now is the time to let go of grudges and anger. Let go of your ego's fixation on needing to win and needing to be right. This is the initiation of a healing process. This is the shedding of weight. This is to grant an amnesty of forgiveness. There does not need to be a sense of winners or losers here. Don't feel like a loser just because you don't feel as though you won. It's not about that. It's about realizing how pointless the battle ever was to begin with. There is only a sense of all this you have been holding onto just doesn't matter. This is to admit that your viewpoints don't need to invalidate another's. This is to call a truce. This is to have your eyes opened so that you can assess the damage. Just as you would examine the damage after a storm, so too do you assess the damage after a conflict.

What forgiveness is being asked of you? Give it. What forgiveness do you expect? Hope for it, but do not demand it. Let it come and accept it if it is offered, but if it is not offered, just let it go. Assume that it is assumed even if it is not presented. To not is only to prolong the battle, to keep the sky dark and not allow the sun to shine. This is a time to reinstate peace. Don't ruin its chances by attaching demands to it.

When embroiled in conflict or engaged in an argument, say to yourself, "What's the point of this?" If there is no point, end it. Let it go. Drop it. It is better to live in peace with calm mind and spirit than to live in a constant storm cloud of your own making. Let the storm end, breathe deeply a breath of forgiveness, and live in peace. This is to master the Five of Swords piece of yourself.

SIX OF SWORDS

We can be so close to our pain that we cannot see it. We just feel it. We know it's there, because there it is. It is a fact of who we are. Figuring out what to do about it can be a challenge, but not as big of a challenge as surrendering to the powers that can help us heal. Sometimes, our egos make it difficult to do that. We want to believe so badly that we can do everything on our own. We want to believe that we have what it takes to get through our problems because we don't want others to see our weaknesses. This is what we tell ourselves. We tell ourselves we can do this because this is what we want to believe.

We try, but no matter how hard we try, we cannot always find the solutions we seek to solve the problems that keep us from being the best versions of our selves. We spin our wheels and no matter what we do, we don't seem to feel any better. We feel sad. We feel depressed. We feel wounded. And we are not imagining these feelings. They are very real, and they affect our lives. They are obstacles, and when we do not do what we know we can do to get past them, they are self-induced obstacles. The way to get past them in order to feel our best is to surrender and accept help from others whom we trust. We need to accept that they have the perspective needed to help us find our way to our personal perfection.

It can be a problem that we are too close to what it is that is bothering us. We have been living with it for so long that maybe we don't even recognize it for what it is anymore. It's just there- what ever it is- and it bothers us. We don't have the broad view to see it with the necessary objectivity to effectively do anything about it. We need help, and we need to accept that simple fact. This is the Six of Swords within us. It is the part of us that says, listen to advice. Allow others to be there for us. Accept help. Let go of pride and admit that we can't do this on our own.

Typically, the six of swords is depicted by a seated figure in a boat. Here is a person hunched over, covered in a blanket. Their face is away from us. We can only imagine the expression on this person's face. Based on the body language and demeanor, it is easy to imagine that this person is not happy. Here is somebody going through a healing process. The blanket they are wrapped in is a cocoon. They have withdrawn into their own world, in need of transformation and healing. They cannot do this alone. They need compassion and understanding. This understanding and compassion is represented by the figure rowing the boat.

Here again, we do not see the face of this person. He is an anonymous figure who only wants to aid this person in the boat. There is no ego involved here. He is not looking at us wanting to be seen, wanting to be known. No, his job is simply to help because he is able to do so and he is needed to do so. There is respect here. He honors this person in his boat. He honors by his simple presence and his willingness to do what is needed without the pursuit of glory. Right now, what is needed is understanding and the strength to row the boat to the shore ahead.

Take note of this shore ahead. The shore ahead is calm. It is peaceful. There is no sign of war or of strife on this land. All seems relaxed and easy going. There are trees growing, and we can imagine the abundance growing there. This is a good place to be. Here, that hooded figure in the boat can heal and become what they need to be. Look at the water they are rowing into. It is calm and mellow, as opposed to the turbulence they are rowing away from. The Six of Swords reminds us that when we have a hard time, when our life gets turbulent, sometimes we need help from others to feel good again. They see the broad picture. They have the advice we need to hear. They know how to get us to that calm land across the water, and by the force of their compassion, they are willing to take us there. We need to let them. It is not a weakness to admit to needing help. A weakness is to need help but to deny it. Strength is to admit to needing help and surrendering to the powers that can provide it. We can set our sights on a distant shore and say, "Over there, I will heal." And then allow ourselves to be taken there.

SEVEN OF SWORDS

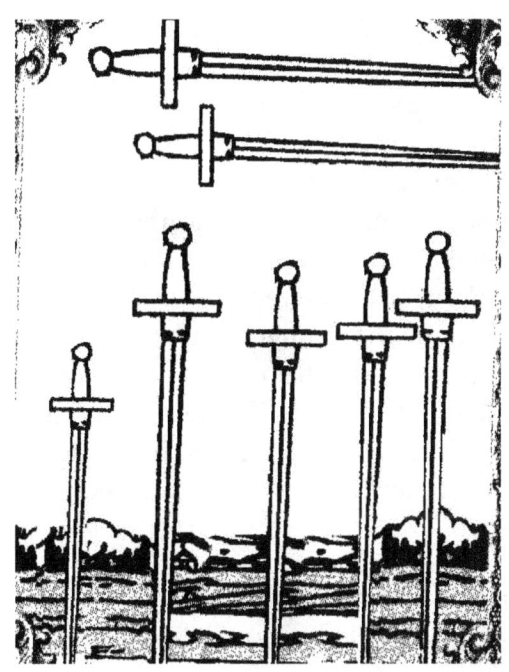

The Seven of Swords is that piece of you that needs to make sure your own needs are being taken care of. And that is a perfectly fine way to feel. As much as people like to act like their own needs are so important, your needs are important too. You have to let others deal with their own issues, wants and desires so you can do the same with yours. If you don't, what's going to happen? You run the risk of deteriorating or falling by the wayside as life passes you by. And for what? So you don't rock the boat and make others feel uncomfortable?

Okay. Let's say you act exactly as others want you to and you don't rock the boat. Let's say you do nothing ever to shake anybody up or make them feel uncomfortable. How do you feel? Do you feel okay? In the interest of balance, is your side of the scale level? If the answer is no, ask yourself why this is. If the answer is because you didn't go for what you wanted and what you needed because you were worried about how somebody else would feel about it, then think about it seriously; are you doing anybody any favors? If you are not getting what is important to you, then how can you be expected to be the best for others?

Think about that safety announcement they make when you fly. They tell you that should the oxygen masks appear, you are to put your own on first before attempting to help anybody else with theirs. But if you care about somebody, shouldn't you make sure they are okay first? Put their needs ahead of your own? That may be your first instinct, on an airplane as well as in other aspects of life, but it is not always the best course of action. This is because you are not much good to anybody if you are in survival mode yourself. In other words, you need to take care of yourself so that you have what it takes to take care of others.

If you are floundering, suffering or struggling, then how much strength do you have for anybody else? It may be in your heart to give people your all when you see that they need it, but if your all is a mere fraction of what it could be, then are you really doing them any real favors? But if you take just a little bit of time to fortify yourself, to gather your strength to be the strongest version of yourself first, then you have so much more to offer. Sometimes to look out for yourself though, you may seem indifferent to others. That's a simple reality. People may see that you are putting yourself first and accuse you of being self-absorbed, self-centered, and selfish. What they don't see is that you are doing this to be the strongest and best version of yourself. If they can just be patient they will see that once you are strong for yourself, you will be there for them and for others. This self-centeredness is just a phase you are going through, and it is important. If you don't go through his phase for yourself, you will never be anything but weak from the needs and demands of others.

What does this do to your authenticity? It can obliterate it if you are not careful. It can create an unhealthy and unnatural balance. Before you know it, you are drowning in somebody else's needs and demands. It can happen that you may even forget who you are. This can push you to a point where in order to remember your true self, you need do some drastic things. You may find yourself acting entirely out of character for yourself just to maintain a sense of self. Living a life where you are always meeting the expectations and demands of others can do this to you. But by being careful to look out for yourself this can be avoided.

In these moments when you really would like to be all you can be for somebody, but circumstances dictate that you must be there for yourself first, it is then that the best you can do is show compassion. Understand what these people are going through and show them some understanding. Let them know what you are going through and hope they can understand. It is okay to expect balance here, and if these other people who expect things from you are unwilling or unable to provide it, then what choice do you have but to force it? Allow yourself to do that. It may seem unnatural and strange to you because it is against your natural impulses, but if this is what you must do, then don't feel bad about doing it. The Seven of Swords piece of you assures you that it is okay.

EIGHT OF SWORDS

The Eight of Swords is that piece of you that would rather hide from an unpleasant truth than face it. This is the piece of you that would rather wear a blindfold and block any of the world's ugliness than take a good look at it. This is the piece of you that would prefer live in denial than face your fears. Why is this? What is it that you fear? It's the same thing we all fear. We fear that which forces us from our comfort zones and makes us face truths that we're more comfortable denying.

We fear disappointment. We fear misunderstandings. We fear pain. We fear fear. We fear having to face the world and deal with the problems in front of us. It is easier to close our eyes and wish them all away. We get conditioned by disappointment and hard times so much that we come to expect them and assume that they are always going to be a part of our lives. This of course, is a fallacy.

We don't always realize when the bad times are behind us. We become so accustomed to them and to our reflexes to them that we react to them as if they are still there. We need to train ourselves to analyze our situations and notice when they have changed and shifted to the better. We need to notice when the difficult times are behind us. If we don't do this, we stay stuck and stagnant in this energy of non-growth, which is based on an untruth.

This untruth is based on the perception that there is an obstacle in our way. But in reality, there is no obstacle. Maybe there used to be, but we have moved past it. What is blocking us now is only just a mirage created by our own minds. Be stronger than your mind. Move past the limits that it sets. Have the courage to charge towards this block with the faith that it will disappear, because it will. It's not real. It is but a shimmer, a mirage. It is nothing but an illusion.

These perceived blocks may become addictions. We may get to a point where we need them to feel normal. Worry, doubt, and fear all become so engrained in our consciousness that we don't know who we are without them. This is unfortunate. This keeps our blinders on and doesn't allow us to see how open and clear the path ahead is. These blinders are not intrinsic to anything actual. You absolutely can move forward; you just need to see that. It is a mindset that makes you feel stuck, so changing that mindset will get you past the block and moving again.

Instead of a mindset of, "I can't go forward," change it to, "There is a way to move forward and I need to just see it." Now you are not being a defeatist. Now you are being positive, and with a positive attitude, things will happen more easily. So, whatever it is that has you feeling stuck, realize that it is all in your head. Realize that the road ahead is open. Realize that the problems are behind you.

It is of great benefit to stop, pause, and take inventory of your circumstances every so often. Take a look at where you are, and how you got there. What obstacles did you overcome? Are there really anymore ahead of you? Be honest with yourself. Are there really any problems ahead? If there are not, relax. Don't spend all your time worrying when there is nothing to worry about. What is the point of that?

While the Eight of Swords is that piece of you that prefers the comfort zone of perceived obstacles, it is also the piece of you that needs to realize that by refusing to move forward based on the perception of these obstacles, you are being stubborn, and this is slowing you down. This stubbornness is keeping you from achieving your greatest and highest good. So for your own sake, and for the sake of those who look up to you and depend on you for guidance and support, rip the blindfold off and take a look behind you. See that anything that was slowing you down is way back there.

You've survived the hardships, and things are better now. Breathe in deep and realize that the road ahead is way smoother than the road behind you. Sure, when you have been through some rough times, it is only natural to still feel slight pangs of anxiety, but do realize this- those pangs are only memories. They are holdovers from what you have been through, not harbingers of what is to come. Now look forward. The path ahead is wide open. Travel it with confidence.

NINE OF SWORDS

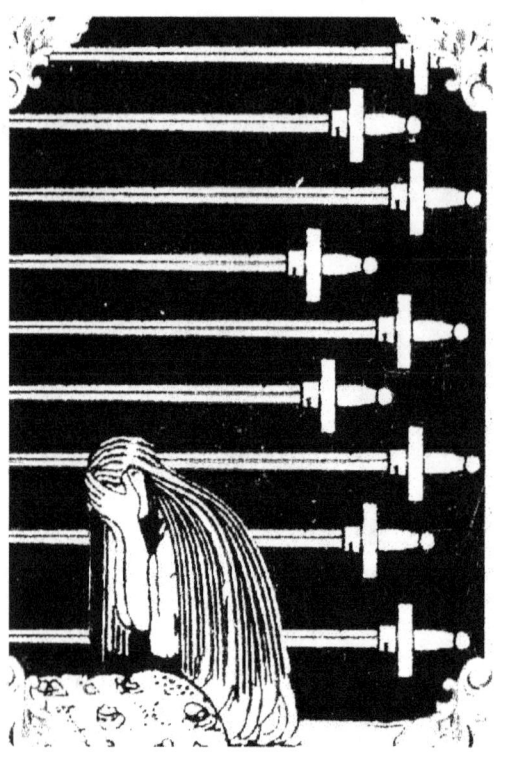

The Nine of Swords is the piece of you that needs to vent frustrations, anger, upsets, and grievances every so often. If you don't let these things out a little at a time as they occur, they will build up and you may suffer a break down. What will this break down look like? It may be a solitary affair where you hide away and avoid the world as you go through what we need to go through. It may be that you snap at and actually attack others. It may be that you become grumpy and stop caring about things you once cared deeply about. None of this is productive and they tend to hurt people who don't deserve to be hurt.

It is natural to be affected by what is going on around you. Most of the time, these things are probably neutral. Whatever is going on in your presence is so benign that you don't even notice it, and you are affected in neither a positive nor negative way. Sometimes what is going on around you is positive and you find yourself feeling good from it. Other times though, you are forced to endure negativity. The things happening around you are getting on your nerves or making you angry or agitated. Frustration can build and you find yourself feeling worse and worse. This negativity happening over time, can build up in detrimental ways. It is in these moments that it is said that you are "triggered."

We are triggered by what is opposite about ourselves, as demonstrated by another person or situation to the point that we find it offensive and bothersome. For example, if you are a quiet person, you may be triggered by a noisy person. If you are, based on your own needs for a quiet environment, somebody who respects the need others have to enjoy their quiet time, it makes sense to you that the world retains orderliness by respecting a person's need for quiet. But then somebody comes along who clearly does not share that value. They are loud, and by your standards, disruptive. This is done in violation of your personal code and no reparations are made. This results in angry feelings. You may suppress this angry feeling for the sake of civility, and this takes energy. That energy builds up and you want to lash out, but you don't. You don't want to make a scene or be thought badly of. So you take a deep breath and let it go. But it doesn't really go anywhere. It is still in you where you left it. This results in stress.

When feeling stressed, make the feelings of stress work for you. When something or somebody bothers you, appreciate it for the chance it offers to learn about yourself. Figure out what the botheration is made of. When you do this, you take charge of the botheration rather than become a victim of it. This puts you in control. Now you can trace that bothered feeling to its source inside of you and take note of what you learn about yourself.

It can though, all add up to be too much to deal with. To prevent that from happening, instead of letting all the stress, pressure, and negativity build up, find ways to purge it in small unobtrusive ways as it manifests inside of you. Instead of blowing up, how about channeling it into something creative? A poem, maybe? A short story? Maybe go for a walk or a swim, or perhaps work out at the gym. Do anything constructive to shake off the negative feelings. Escape. Watch a movie. Read a novel. Take a long walk in nature. Do whatever it takes to get out of your head and escape the thoughts that are eating at you. Ask yourself, "How does it serve me to be locked in this prison of my own mind with these thoughts that are driving me crazy?" Then step away from them. When you come back to them, how are they different? Do they still have the same power over you, or have they diminished? Don't let your own thoughts drive you crazy.

When you shift energy from negative and vindictive into something useful, you are the master of your own soul. You are not letting negative input chart the course of your day. You are turning the tables and creating a positive outcome. You are not going to be defeated by negativity. You have made friends with your frustrations and angers and have mastered the art of self control. When you accomplish this, life becomes so much simpler.

TEN OF SWORDS

The Ten of Swords is that piece of you that is filled with a sense of desperation and despair. To be experiencing the Ten of Swords is to be downed by the pressures of life. It is as if you have been stabbed. Not just stabbed, but stabbed multiple times with the very sharp swords of your own mind. You have been left bleeding by these swords. You have been left bleeding with the viscous gore of your sanity leaking out of every point of impact from these swords. Or maybe your brain has exploded. Maybe each and every stressful thought was a lightning bolt that has struck your brain and caused it to destruct. Whatever the case may be, the result is the same. There's a good chance that you are dead. What exactly happened here?

To understand what happened here, keep in mind that the suit of swords represent your thoughts and the affect your own mind has on you. Thinking about that, look at what your own thoughts are capable of doing to you. Remember, these are your thoughts, and not anybody else's. These are your thoughts, attitudes, actions, and reactions. This is what you did to yourself by letting your thoughts get away from you. This is what happens when you let yourself get stressed out. The rest of your body just can't take what your mind is doing as it produces all that hardship and negativity, so it has a breakdown. It puts itself into survival mode and acts in ways that are uncharacteristic for it. It clearly needs help to be its normal self again. This is not the end of the world. It is just a temporary situation brought on by stress.

Stress and worry can be overwhelming. Your thoughts can get out of control and the burden of thinking too much kills you. You don't always realize you are doing this to yourself until the deed is done and you are dead. The good thing about being dead though, is that it opens the door for rebirth, because once you are dead, you are not going to get any deader. Dead is definite. As dead as you are is as dead as you are going to be. It's not going to get any worse, and because it is not going to get any worse, you can analyze what exactly happened and make it better.

Recognize stressful feelings as warnings of what is ahead if you don't change your attitude and your thoughts. This current path is leading you to a downfall. Understanding this: you know you should change some things in your life as to prevent this crash. It is a crash of your own making. It is a crash brought on by your own rigid thinking and unwillingness to change. Really examine what your thoughts did to you, and send healing energy to the wounded parts so you can get back up, shake off the hurt and live again. When you do this, you are that much stronger.

It helps to remember that when you crash, things can only get better. That's what happens when you finally hit the bottom, and that is what happens when you let your thoughts dominate and control your life. They will eventually drive you crazy. Once they drive you crazy, you can settle down and look for sanity again. What's been bothering you lately? What's been on your mind? Just stop thinking, stop seeking, stop reacting, and take inventory of your thoughts and your attitudes. Which ones are taking you down the dangerous path? Change them. Alter them from destructive to constructive. Look for something good instead of dwelling on anything bad. Look for solutions to problems; don't just dwell on the problems themselves.

You will see the difference it makes to finally turn things around and begin the healing process. Having crashed, hit the bottom, been stabbed by swords of your own making puts you in a unique position. This is where you surrender to your pain and stop denying it. Denial does not make it go away. Accepting it so you can determine a course of action to overcome it is ultimately what heals it. So there you are. Remove those swords, heal yourself, and remember the lesson that is to be learned from it all. That is, do your best to not let things get to you. Stay as positive as you are possibly able to be and find constructive ways to deal with stress. When you do this, the Ten of Swords are not so sharp anymore.

PAGE OF SWORDS

The Page of Swords is your inner child, curious and astute. This is the piece of you that has a thirst to learn. This is the piece of you that has discovered a new subject and wants to know as much about it as is possible. This is the piece of you that loves researching, understanding, and asking questions in order to gain new knowledge and understanding.

Imagine a very young person, just starting out in the world. They have much that they don't understand, but they want to learn. They will put in the effort to track down the information they want, no matter what it takes. In so doing, they may cross lines or disrespect personal boundaries, or at least it may seem like they are. But in their own minds, they are not. Their intentions are pure. They do not mean to step on anybody's toes or bother anybody. They see the world as a cooperative unit where we all work together to help each other out and share knowledge and wisdom and appreciate honesty and directness. They are not content to merely accept things at face value; they want to comprehend concepts and principles at their core. This young person is you. This is the piece of you that wants to learn it all.

Indulge your inner Page of Swords by indulging your innate curiosity. Ask all the questions you have, and then think up a few more and ask those too. Explore the new things you have had your mind set on exploring but just never did. Just do it. Don't hold back and don't back off. Don't say no to your inner child when he/she wants answers. Seek out these answers and enjoy the process of doing so. When you leave your inhibitions behind you and seek answers, you expand your spirit, because you are not placing conditions on yourself as to how and what you should learn. Get past the idea that you know it all already, because you don't and you never will. So be like a child with infinite curiosity and see what new things you can learn. Make it fun. Make it exciting. Maybe even make it dangerous.

As a communicator, the Page of Swords doesn't always employ empathy or compassion with their choice of words. If it is on their mind to say it, they say it without thinking twice about it. And why should they? If they have something to say, they say it in just the way they think it. They have an "Out of the mouths of babes and sucklings" quality to them. If it pops into their minds, chances are it will come out their mouth, unfiltered. Some may feel that they talk too much, and perhaps they do. This need not be considered a negative quality. It is only negative to those who would rather not have to listen to them, but such things are arbitrary and different from person to person. There is a certain freedom and strength to being confident and able to say what is on your mind, how it is on your mind, and when it is on you without worrying about what anybody will think of you for it.

The Page of Swords is synonymous with the Fool with a sharp mind. Just as the Fool represents a primal beginning and a journey of faith, the Page of Swords represents a new intellectual journey. This is a journey of learning, interpreting, and understanding. The Page of Swords is the piece of you that can't get enough of that sort of thing.

KNIGHT OF SWORDS

The Knight of Swords is that piece of you that is direct and to the point. This is the piece of you that has little time for trifling matters or for pandering to those who lack self-confidence. When you see that there is a need for somebody to take control of a situation, this is the piece of you that has no trouble stepping up and doing so. You are bold, courageous, and adventurous.

As a bold, courageous and adventurous person, you tend to have a big personality. You can be loud and probably don't notice if you are being a bother to others. You have the confidence to say what is on your mind but lack the empathy and compassion to stifle yourself when people don't want or need to hear it. You act on impulses and don't hold back or assess the impact your actions will have on others. You put your own needs first and are prone to speaking without filters. You may not slow down to take into account how other people feel about your actions or how your words will sink into them and make them feel. As you act on your immediate impulses, you may come across as pushy, abrasive, and annoying.

The Knight of Swords within you, though, means no harm. This piece of you simply lacks awareness of the space others need and the peace they are trying to hold onto. You don't recognize how your actions give other people the sensation that swords are jabbing into the various lobes of their brain causing discomfort, distress, and discombobulation. And this is what they will remember about you. Behavior leads to impressions. Impressions generate expectations. The way you treat somebody or the way you act around them will create the expectation they have of you. If you act negatively, they will expect an unpleasant encounter with you the next time they see you. Even the mention of your name may create a negative reaction within them. If though your actions towards them are positive, they will expect a positive interaction with you. The mention of your name may trigger a happy and positive reaction.

The Knight of Swords piece of you has numerous positive traits that people will appreciate. One of those positive traits is your ability to give a voice to those who have a hard time being heard, because sometimes to feel empowered, that's all a person really wants- to be heard and to have a voice. Maybe they need an advocate or a spokesperson because they simply don't know how to speak up or what exactly to say if they did. Maybe through an advocate or a spokesperson they will find their voice and their power. This is to be a positive force as you tap into your inner Knight of Swords. If you find that you are in a position to empower somebody by giving them a voice, do so. The difference that can make in somebody's life can be unprecedented.

As a communicator, the Knight of Swords will say whatever they need to say or what somebody wants to hear to get their own way. They are not always honest. They do not have the purity of the Page of Swords, nor the maturity of a Queen or King. They haven't yet learned that they can get more by being truthful and honest than by being dishonest. When they are honest though, they are straight to the point. They will answer your questions directly without a "Ha ha, aren't I so clever" kind of answer or in a way that makes you wonder what they mean.

The Knight of Swords piece of you is charged up and energetic. It is ready to charge forward without the benefit of caution. It is impulsive and demanding. These are great qualities when there are things that need doing and somebody needs to take charge. These can be annoying qualities when they manifest as control-freakism. The Knight of Swords represents that quality in you that knows what it wants and goes for it, no matter what.

QUEEN OF SWORDS

The Queen of Swords is that piece of you that is a clear-headed, logical, and rational thinker. When all about you is losing theirs, you manage to keep your wits about you. When an answer is needed, you give one that is precise and to the point. You don't convolute your communication with a lot of gobbledygook or pointless rambling. No, you get to the point, and you do so with confidence. You take on leadership roles, and your intuition and empathy make you an ideal collaborator. People seek you out for your straightforwardness and your ability to deliver any message to any audience, even if it is a difficult message to deliver. The Queen of Swords in you has a natural understanding of diversity and knows how to relate to, motivate, and communicate with about everybody.

Your Queen of Swords aspect is essentially the High Priestess with a sharp mind. Just as the High Priestess delivers her messages in a direct and to the point manner, so to do you without letting emotions get in the way. It is not that you do not feel emotions, it is just that you will not let them get in the way of clarity. When there is something that needs to be said, you say it. You don't lose the message to unnecessary words or convolute it with forgettable utterances. You don't beat around the bush and force people to figure out what you mean. Because of this, you are respected for your skills at collecting and disseminating information.

As a communicator, your inner Queen of Swords is concise. Before you talk, you know exactly what you want to say, or at least you come across as though you do. This is a gift. There is such a thing as word pollution. It is so easy to add so much extra stuff that doesn't need to be said to any particular message, that the true meaning of your true message gets lost to it all. So, the fact that you say just what needs saying and leave the rest unsaid is a gift to those who don't have to wade through and filter out all the extraneous blather. You are concise, honest, and truthful.

Sometimes, things are way less perfect than we want them to be. When this is the case, there may be bad news to deliver, and somebody needs to be the messenger. The best messengers are those with compassion and understanding, who can tempered the news with compassion so that it is easier to hear. Ask yourself how you would like to hear this. Then deliver it accordingly. This is your true Queen of Swords quality- the ability to say what needs saying even when it is hard to say. This is the Queen of Swords' communication style, to be direct and to the point.

As much as your Queen of Swords aspect is appreciated for its directness, it can at times create the impression that you are cold and aloof. That is to be expected. When you have to be direct without letting your emotions get in the way, it is bound to happen that people will think you do not have emotions and that you are cold and distant. You know better though. You know you are just as thoughtful, compassionate, empathetic, and loving as anybody else. Just because you have a knack for transcending personal feelings and needs for the sake of others doesn't mean you feel nothing. It just means you have a unique talent for not letting your personal feelings get in the way when others depend on you. To master this is a gift is to be a master of the world you are in. If you have mastered this, be grateful for that Queen of Swords piece of you that has enabled this quality within you.

KING OF SWORDS

You don't have anything to prove to anybody, yet you are more than happy to help with clear answers, advice, the benefit of your experience, and your ability to apply logic. You know that success is not in only what you achieve for yourself, but in how you influence others and facilitate their success as well, and you want others to succeed. What doors can you open for others? What lights can you lead others to? These questions are frequently on your mind. This is the King of Swords in you. This is the piece of you that is in its natural element when engaged in intellectual and mental pursuits.

As the King of Swords, you do not let negative people dictate to you what kind of a day you will have or what mood you will be in. You are able to ascend above the bad moods and negativity of others. You float above it all and maintain who you are no matter what others may try to get you to be. You don't sink into a bad mood because that is what everybody else is in. No, you maintain your own sense of self no matter what the dominate sensation are in the room.

You know what your strengths and your powers are. You know the power of your mind, and you are not afraid to use it, but you certainly do not have any need to show off. People may project onto you their ideas of what they think you are. They may assume that because you are as smart and knowledgeable as you are that you must be full of yourself, or have an attitude about it. The reality is though, you don't. You are just being yourself and letting others conform their selves around who you are. If they want to jump to the conclusion that you think a lot of yourself, that is their business. It is too bad for them if they don't let you be yourself out of a misplaced notion of your grandiose stature.

Expect people to assume you are the authority on whatever the case at hand is. In reality, you may or may not be the authority, but because people seem to think you are, you better have some answers. If you don't have the answers, you better know where they can be found. As long as you are not wishy-washy on any questions that come up, as long as you can definitely answer it, or definitely say "I don't know" without making people guess what you mean, you will garner respect.

In emergency situations, stressful times, or just times of change, people look for a leader. They need somebody to infuse the situation with fresh ideas and new energy. It would seem that you are that somebody. Give the people what they want. You see things differently than they do. You offer a fresh perspective. You take control and show the people a new path. There may be tough decisions to make, and you make them confidently. You make them based on what is best for everybody, while putting your ego aside and focus on the needs of the group.

When things have been the same way for too long, the paradigm grows stale. Here again, somebody needs to step up and rock the stagnation until the energy is flowing again. That's what happens. You get a group of people together for a specific function, and at first it goes well. But then complacency sets in. The group gets so stuck in the idea of how everything should be done that they do not take into account the subtle (or not subtle) changes that come about. So growth is hindered. Somebody with a holistic view of it all needs to step in and shake things up and get the energy flowing again. You, as the King of Swords, are that somebody.

As the King of Swords, your communication style is mature, honest, and direct. You know what you need to say, and you say it with authority and conviction. Because of your maturity and honesty, people trust you. Your word is golden.

That King of Swords quality in you will serve you well anytime the power of intellect is called for. It gives you the upper hand in times when a decisive and definite decision or opinion is needed.

Part Three: Pentacles

The pieces of ourselves related to our materialism

ACE OF PENTACLES

You possess the seed of abundance. You know this. But what are you doing with it? Are you intellectualizing about it, or are you actually planting it, nurturing it, taking care of it, encouraging it to grow? Don't just think, if I did this… I should do this… If I did such and such a thing, such and such would be the result. What do you expect to get out of this? Do you think that everything magically happens just because you think about it? That's not how it works. Results don't come from wishful thinking. Results come from actions. So get busy. Turn your intellectualizations into actions into results. You have what it takes to create your abundance. This is a piece of who you are. It is your inner Ace of Pentacles.

Think in terms of potential energy. Here is something that could easily happen, but you must supply the right conditions for it. You have ideas and resources. Combined, these ideas and resources can easily turn into something beneficial and lucrative. So, make it happen. Think of this potential energy in terms of a kernel of popcorn. Stored inside that kernel is the potential to pop and turn into something quite different from that little kernel. But it is not going to pop spontaneously without any help. You need to provide the proper conditions, grease in a pan (if you are old school about it) and the right amount of heat. The point is, it takes conscious effort. What kernel of potential do you have stored in your mind? Throw some grease on it and turn up the heat. Watch it pop. Watch it turn into something a whole lot better than what it was when it started.

Inspiration is all around you and from this inspiration, fortune can evolve. How many times have you heard somebody say, "Wouldn't it be great if somebody did this…" or "I just had a great idea for…." Or, "I just had a great idea for a movie...." and then they let it go at that. They have these great ideas but no willingness to follow through. That is unfortunate for them. A burst of inspiration followed up on by action is what brings great new things to the world, and with the just the right marketing, it can bring to the one who created it, good fortune. Think about that as inspiration hits you. Think about your inner Ace of Pentacles and realize just how good of a thing this can be, and how good it can be for you for it to be it actualized. Ideas are great. But when as far as they get is your own head, they do not do the world much good.

Examine the ideas that keep coming back to you, the ones you can't shake, especially the one that seems too impossible to implement, so you push them away. Give these ideas some thought. They are not impossible. You just haven't found that push to make them happen. Let that change. As these ideas come back to you, see if they bring with them new ideas on how to make them happen. Think of these idea as seeds of prosperity. Plant these seeds, nurture them, and watch them grow. When it has grown, marvel at what it has brought into your life by way of prosperity and abundance. You have what it takes, so stay focused on it.

Your inner Ace of Pentacles is your raw, primordial spark of success. What you do with it is up to you. Nurture it and give it what it needs to grow, and you will enjoy its benefits. That's what it is there for. It is not there to tease you and say, "Look at these great ideas you have. Too bad you can't do anything with them." No. It is there to say, "Success is yours for the taking, so take it." Listen to that and make it happen

TWO OF PENTACLES

The Two of Pentacles is that piece of you that maintains vigilance and balance. It maintains vigilance to see that balance is maintained. It maintains balance so that vigilance is in order. It is a juggling act for the sake of equilibrium. There may be too much of one element, but not enough of the other. Or vice-versa. The challenge is to keep these components in check with one another so that one does not dominate and overshadow the other. This is nothing new to your inner Two of Pentacles. These acrobatics have been going on pretty much forever. It becomes so much a part of who you are that you barely notice it anymore, until the balance becomes too far out of whack and you must struggle to correct it.

Your Two of Pentacles sees the laws of cause and effect. When you do one thing, a predictable consequence occurs. If you don't do that one thing, something else entirely happens. Do any number of other things, and a variety of other results will ensue. The question becomes, what do you want the end result to be? Focus on what you must do to make that happen. As you do this, how is the balance of the other elements in your life effected?

For example, if you spend a great deal of money on a boat for your leisure, how does that effect your mortgage payment? Can you still pay it on time? You knew what you were getting yourself into when you bought the boat. Are you causing yourself hardship now because of it? If you had not have bought the boat, would you have put that money towards something different, of would you have been practical with it? This piece of you knows to think things through and consider what the end result will mean to you in the material world.

Your Two of Pentacles knows better than to put all your eggs in one basket, and not putting your hopes and faith in one entity. There is a reality to the fact that things do not always work out exactly as planned. You may have high hopes for one thing, a job for example. Suppose you interviewed for a job you would love to have, and you really hope to get it. Are you prepared for possibility that you might not? It's a good idea to be. Apply for other jobs just in case, because who knows what to expect. Know what Plan B will be in case you need it. Know what Plan C will be in case you need that too. Always think ahead. Always have a contingency plan in case the initial plan does not work out.

This piece of you is prepared to multitask, because life can be a juggling act. Just to stay on track and stay balanced, sometimes you have to take on a lot of different things at once. You need to stay aware of how focusing your energy on one element of your life is effecting the others. You need to make sure you are not losing sight of one element as attention is so focused on another. Don't let your guard down. Constantly monitor the situation so alterations can be made on the spot and in the moment to not let one situation or another get out of hand. Always assess and anticipate the next move so you don't get too far behind. This is a constant act of balancing, and it's what the Two of Pentacles within you is made for.

Think of your Two of Pentacles as the Temperance card of the material world. Whereas Temperance is focused on the energetic balance of life, the Two of Pentacles is focused on material balance. What balance do you need to stay centered and grounded on the earth? What do these balances mean to you as a worldly being, rooted in the material world? Remember, you are a being of the material world. No matter how spiritual you consider yourself, your feet are on the ground and you need materialism to survive. Your Two of Pentacles knows this and is focused on maintaining the necessities of earth-bound life.

THREE OF PENTACLES

There is a saying, "Many hands make light work." This is the attitude of your inner Three of Pentacles. Sometimes, yes, you want to work alone and do your own thing. But sometimes team work is better. Sometimes it is necessary. Sometimes, if you want to get paid, you have to endure it whether you want to or not. So, work together. Get down with some group dynamics to generate some team synergy so that what you are working on will come together in a worthwhile way.

Working with others can also test your ego and your ability to fit in with others. Even a natural born leader must be willing to be a follower sometimes. Even a follower must be willing and able to step up and be a leader when needed. Group dynamics and team work grant you the opportunity to figure out where you fit into the whole, because you don't always know, do you? It may change from group to group and situation to situation.

Different groups require you to find different reserves within yourself. Every group has a different variety of people. Your place within each group may change when in different groups. Even if you are a leader, how willing are the others to follow? Have you gained their respect and trust? Examine how you feel about them. Decide who you feel comfortable around and who you have connections with. Notice the ones that make you feel uncomfortable to whatever level of discomfort they create in you, and consider their personality and why they make you feel that way.

Do you go blindly go along with what is happening, or do you question leadership? It changes from group to group and from task to task. How willing and able are you to bend, change, and adapt as the situation demands? You may find that you are uncomfortable or unwilling to take orders. You may discover that you are not comfortable giving orders. Each group you find yourself in will bring with it its own set of tests and revelations about yourself. The people you enjoy being around, appreciate them. Those you do not, do your best to put up with them. Those you are neutral towards, accept them.

If the leadership you are working for bothers you, seek to understand why. Maybe it is that you feel these people are unqualified to lead. Maybe you have a personal grudge against them. Perhaps they have rubbed you the wrong way about something or other in the past. Or it could be that you don't agree with their vision for the project. Take your feelings of discomfort and use them as a catalyst for self understanding as you seek to define what it is you don't like and what you would do differently.

When you are the leader, maintain an air of credibility, authority, and respectability. Lead for the good of the team and the project. Do your best not to let your ego and personal feelings get in the way of being the way-seer for the group. Keep your eye on end results and take the ideas and opinions of the group to heart. To lead, you need not be a dictator, but rather the filter through whom decisions are made. A leader needs to be accountable for the decisions that are made, but not necessarily make these decisions in a vacuum. A leader needs to consider the input of the team, and make the ultimate decision.

The Three of Pentacles in you is the piece that is not alone in a void. It is connected to others in pursuit of a common goal. This is the piece of you that gets to explore who it is in relation to who others are. It gets to gather strength through what it learns of itself by taking note of how it feels in different group dynamics. This is the piece of you that is a piece of the collective.

FOUR OF PENTACLES

The Four of Pentacles is that piece of you that can be clingy sometimes. It's that piece of you that has a hard time letting go. There is security in holding on. There is comfort in familiarity. This is what the Four of Pentacles in you is clinging to. It is clinging to what it understands and is predictable so it doesn't have to reinvent itself with new and unfamiliar entities. It clings so that life maintains a sense of constancy and consistency. This piece of you doesn't always want to have to guess abut new things. It doesn't want to figure out how to fit the unfamiliar into its paradigm. It wants the peace that prior understanding brings.

The Four of Pentacles clings to what gives it a sense of security. It fears loss. It fears letting go, because what if it lets go and nothing fills in the gap that is left behind? Here, it must have faith. It must have faith that all it needs will be provided. However, it must make room for it. How does it make room when it maintains clutter?

The Four of Pentacles hangs on to grudges and pain, convincing itself that there is some intrinsic value to it. But what is the reality? The reality is that these things are not meant to stay within us. Don't allow negativity and old, stagnant energy to take up all the space that could just as easily be taken up with positivity and new energy. Appreciate what each and everything that comes into your life has to offer, and then be prepared to release it when its purpose has been served. Don't let fear make you feel that nothing new will ever come in.

The Four of Pentacles needs to understand that it is okay to let go. Not everything needs to be held onto. There are a great number of things that come to us in life that are meant to be utilized in the moment, for a time. They are not meant to be held onto forever. So be okay with letting go. You'll never grow if you don't. If you hold onto to everything, you will be too weighed down to effectively continue on to future chapters of your life.

The question can become though, and easily so, "Don't I need to hold onto some things? Isn't that okay?" The only logical answer is, "Yes. Of course." The trick is to be discerning and honest with yourself about what those things are. Ask yourself if such and such a thing still has value. Do you utilize it, is it important to you in the now and will it potentially be in some potential future? If the answer is yes, then yes of course. It is still of value. If you cannot, in all honesty, see any utilization of it, then let it go. You are done with it. It has completed its purpose in your life.

The Four of Pentacles maintains a balancing act all of its own. It is charged with discriminating between what is valuable and important and what it is not. It is its job to evaluate and determine what to keep and what to discard. Trust its judgment. Listen to what it has to tell you. Letting go means being light. Being light means being free. Free yourself. Let go. Relive yourself of the burden of excessive baggage. Your life will be that much simpler for it.

FIVE OF PENTACLES

There is that feeling of being left behind, like everybody has moved on, but they forgot about you. Now you are left out. Now you wonder what you should do. It feels like being outside in the cold while everybody else is inside where it is warm, enjoying pleasant company and good fellowship. The piece of you that feels this is the Five of Pentacles. It has a general sense of lack and poverty.

There are basic needs we all have to remain alive. There is nutrition, water, shelter, all that kind of stuff. But just being alive doesn't mean you are living. There is a lot more to life than just these rudimentary basics. We want, and are entitled to, comforts. We like to have a nice place to live. We like to eat the food we like to eat and sleep in comfortable accommodations. We like space to put our stuff that we can call our own. This is a step up from merely being alive, to having a place in society. Many people like to have nice TVs and cars. And why shouldn't they? If this brings about happiness, is there any reason not to pursue it?

Pursuing luxuries and comforts can actually give you a sense of purpose in your life. If you want something bigger and better than what you have, you need a plan to go about getting it. You need to earn it. Finding ways to earn it puts you on a course to contribute to society as you find ways to earn more money, seeking employment and things to do that will earn you money. By earning money and spending it on the things you want, whether you "need" them or not keeps the economy alive. So do that. Save up and buy anything that makes you happy to have. You are entitled to it.

It can happen though that to not have the nice things and comforts that you want will make you feel poor. Are you poor though? Be honest with yourself. Do you have what you need? Are you just upset about what you want but cannot have? It's a normal feeling, but are you going to let it define you? Take a look at what you have and be happy to have it without feeling like a second class citizen or a victim of circumstances. Are you comparing yourself to somebody else and wishing you had what they have? Do you watch nicer cars going by than the one you are driving, and wish you had that too? Don't.

Don't unless you plan to put your money away until one day you can say "It is mine!" This car is just one example. There are countless others. Don't look at somebody else's house and wish you could live in such a place unless wishing this enacts within you a drive to strive for more. Don't stand outside a fancy restaurant looking inside at the gourmet food other people are eating, feeling hungry, unless that food is prompting you to look for a better job that will allow you to make such eateries a regular part of your own existence.

The Five of Pentacles within you is there to prompt you to aim higher if you are discontent with your life circumstances. It is telling you to not settle for less if you are not content with less. It is telling not to complain about your life, but to work at making the changes that will bring your life up to the par you want it to be. It is telling you to not feel like less of a person because somebody else has the things you want but cannot afford to have, but to activate your power to generate your own riches.

SIX OF PENTACLES

The Six of Pentacles within you both sees the value in others, and appreciates feeling valued itself. A feeling of value is something we all need. We need to know that we are appreciated and seen. We need to know that what matters to us matters at all, and that the fact that we care makes a difference. We need to know that our voice is heard and that people care what we have to say. We need to know that in our times of need, we are not alone. A sense of value gives us each the energy to keep on keeping on and to persevere through life's challenges.

When you sense that somebody is in need, decide what things you can do, whether large or small, that will make them feel that life is worthwhile. Somebody may need financial help. Can you help them out? Offer some of what you have to help them through a difficult time? Do this with a generous spirit without the demand that you get anything in return for it, unless it is meaningful to them to know that they can repay you at a later date. If it is important to them to be able even up with you when they can, let them do so. But don't force the issue. Let it flow naturally.

Maybe what somebody needs is a hug. Let's face reality, a hug from the right person can go a long way. A hug is a heart to heart connection that is better than a handshake. In the right time and the right place, it is therapeutic. It is an offering of your energy straight from the source. A hug should not be forced. Not everybody wants them all the time, but when one from you can make a difference, don't hold back.

Sometimes a person needs to be heard. We all have something to say. But who's listening? Anybody? Knowing somebody somewhere is listening offers a sense of validity. It tells a person that they are worthwhile. To feel like nobody cares and nobody is listening is to have low self esteem and feelings of inadequacies. And why wouldn't it? We all have things to say and reasons for saying it. It's only natural to feel devalued if nobody is paying attention. So listen to people. Let them communicate. Let them express their selves. Hear what they are saying. Value them that much.

What a person might need is to be seen. Eye contact achieves this. When you are talking to somebody, and they are talking to you, be sure to look them in the eye. This establishes a connection and lets them know that you are not simply humoring them, but are genuinely interested in what they have to say. This gives a sense of being more than just being tolerated, but cared about. This is an important facet of communication. It gives a sense of oneness, and it is so simple. Just look at them. Easy as that.

The Six of Pentacles is that piece of you that sees value of other beings, thus being willing to help them see their own value and feel appreciated. Sometimes things happen that are out of our control: losses, deaths of loved ones, natural disasters that take us from all that we own and hold dear. This puts us into survival mode where we must struggle to maintain a sense of value and of self. Your generosity and kindness could very well go a long way with this, so don't hesitate to give. When in need yourself, accept what others will offer you. Don't be too proud to receive. Life is a matter of give and take, take and give, spread it around, receive and offer. It all depends where you are in the cycle of all such things whether you are in a position to accept or give. Just be open to whatever is necessary.

SEVEN OF PENTACLES

Waiting for success

can be boring. Let's face reality. It can be. The Seven of Pentacles piece of you is used to it though. This is the piece of you that has long had to endure patience it wishes it didn't have to endure. This is the piece of you that wants to fast forward past all the boring "It takes time" part of the actualization process and get to the good stuff at the end of the wait. But life is not like that. Life is all about planting seeds and waiting for them to grow. Life is about allowing for the natural processes and laws of reality to take place. Things don't always happen instantaneously. More often than not, you have to wait.

But if you believe in what you are doing and what you know you will accomplish, you just have to put up with being bored and with waiting. Remember when you were just starting out and you dreamed of what success would look like. Now notice how much you have done since then. Notice you actually have come quite far. So, don't let yourself feel down for not being there yet. You're getting there a step at a time. Is it going slower than you had hoped? Well, what exactly where your hopes? You know things take awhile, and anything worthwhile is worth putting in the time and effort to achieve. So keep putting in the time. Keep putting in the effort. Before you know it, you will have achieved. When you plant a seed, do you expect a full grown plant to pop up overnight? Of course not. You need to water and nurture it and give it what it needs to prosper.

Imagine you are baking cookies. You would leave them in the oven until they are done, because if you take them out too soon, they won't be any good, and if you like cookies, that is not going to be acceptable. The same goes with cooking chicken. You want that to be cooked all the way before you eat it, or you run the risk of getting all kinds of sick from it. And how about boiling an egg? You can't just boil an egg a little bit. What kind of a mess is that going to be when you crack it open? No, you have to boil it all the way if you are going to boil it at all. That's just how life is.

Impatience will not do you any good. Things are going to happen in the time they are going to happen no matter what, so why rush them? Somethings you can control, sure. But what about those things you cannot? Are you really going to let them drive you crazy? It is all about your thoughts about whatever is going on. So, if there is something you are waiting for to happen, but you are unable to make this happen any faster than it is going to, what's the point of getting upset or stressing out over it? This is all in your head and in your attitude.

Change your thinking from wishing things would go faster to an attitude of, "This will take a while, and that is okay. I will give it the time it needs." Then do that. Give it time. Give it all the time it needs. You can't change the time it takes, you can only change your attitude about it. So any stress you feel about how long something takes to happen is brought on by yourself. It is your choice. Listen to the Seven of Pentacles when it tells you to be patient.

EIGHT OF PENTACLES

The Eight of Pentacles within you appreciates the power of predictability. When you know what to expect, and what is expected of you, you can get into a steady routine and get things done. There is no guess work here. No trial and error. No experimentation. You know what needs doing so you do it. When your thoughts are not focused on the task at hand because you know what you are doing and you are in the zone, you are free to daydream. You are free to let your mind wander into other realms where solutions to problems you are dealing with can be found. You will also find inspirations for other projects, ideas for your life in general, and entire plateaus of other dimensions to mentally explore. So get into your routine, slip into autopilot, and take a stroll through your mind.

Your inner Eight of Pentacles knows what it means to have work to do. And it doesn't mind doing it. Why fight it? This piece of you knows that it is futile to resist. You can't put off whatever you need to do forever, so you might as well wrap your mind around the task and get through it. Appreciate the rewards that come with completion. A paycheck, maybe. Improvements to your environment, perhaps. Maybe the appreciation of others, even. Who knows? It could even be that finishing this task creates opportunities later to have a good time.

Sometimes life is about good times and having fun. Other times it is about getting down to business and getting done what needs to be gotten done so you can have the time and resources to have those fun and good times later. You need to get focused and be methodical. Concentrate on what the ultimate goal is, then gear your actions towards accomplishing that. The best way to do this is to eliminate distractions. Focus. Work hard. Get it done.

Sometimes this is just what you have to do. Sometimes you have to be result oriented. There is satisfaction in seeing all that you have accomplished.

Get in your groove. Get your work done. Don't feel like you need to create a whole new system to accomplish whatever it is that you need to accomplish. You know what you're doing. You know what works. "If it ain't broke, don't fix it" as some people are fond of saying. What has always worked, will still work. So you are free from the burden of trying to figure out what to do and how to do it. All you have to do, is do it. The sooner you start, the sooner you will be done. It's all good. Just get busy. Before you know it, your work will be done and you can move onto other things. And in the process of doing your work, who knows what thoughts you will think and what inspirations you will find. So get into it and see where it takes you.

NINE OF PENTACLES

You planted that seed of abundance, the Ace of Pentacles. You nurtured it, provided it with light and sustenance, and weeded it to keep it alive and happy. Now, it has grown to fruition. Remember what your intentions were when you planted it? What you saw as its greatest potential? What you imagined as its full maturity? Remember, maintaining patience even when it seemed it was going to take forever before you could enjoy the bounty of your efforts? Well, the time has come. Your efforts to bring it to harvest have paid off. You can now enjoy the fruits that your seed of abundance has provided. This is the Nine of Pentacles within you.

You've worked hard. You've encountered obstacles, setbacks, problems, and through it all, did you lose track of what it is that you are working for? Perhaps you did, but no matter, you managed to get back on track. Now it is time to appreciate what all your efforts were about. Take notice of your abundance. It was through your own efforts and diligence that you achieved this. You made this happen. What exactly did you do? Can you remember all of it? Could you mentor somebody in how they can do it too? Just know that all the work you did was not for nothing. All the work you did has gotten you to where you are now. What you have is a result of your efforts.

What you plant is what you need to plant to become what you want to be. If you want to be thought of as a great writer, you plant the seeds that will grow into success as a writer. You practice at the craft. You take classes to improve your ability. You get feedback from others who have feedback to give. This is how you nurture that great writer seed. Or that great artist seed, if that is your ambition. Or the seed of great parenthood, if you have kids that you endeavor to raise well. Whatever that thing, or those things are to you, that's what you need to plant. So be mindful. Be mindful of how your actions and your intentions become who you are.

Even though you have put your all into your objective, maybe you feel you have not achieved it. In times like these, ask yourself if you have done enough, because if it is still unachieved, maybe you haven't. If there is not an abundance to harvest, maybe you're jumping the gun. Maybe it's not time yet, and you need to have just a little more patience. You may be writing great things, but are you getting it out there to the world to appreciate it? Have you truly dedicated yourself to perfecting the craft of writing? Whatever your dream is, whatever your goal is, walk the walk. Embody what it means to be what you want to be. Embody what it means to be how you want to be. Do this all encompassingly- mind, body and soul. When you know that this is what you are, it is what you become.

If you don't feel that you are what you had hoped to become, trace your steps backwards to figure out what you planted to achieve the harvest you ended up with. You may find certain things that you don't remember planting. You may ask yourself where these things came from. Trace your steps backwards to figure out what you did to bring about the harvest you got. What did you graft onto the original planting to grow into what you ended up with? What else did you plant that has now grown along with your intend growth?

You may have had one intention, but by the time to harvest the bounty came along, you discover something completely different has grown, and you like it. Pay attention to this. This tells you something about who you are that you probably didn't know before. This may even change your original ambition. This opens the door to discover that there are things within you that you did not yet know about, certain seeds that are only just now sprouting. Now that you do know of them, you have a new plateau to explore, and new interests to foster. Why not see where they take you? The nine of pentacles within you recognizes the culmination of your efforts. Whether you feel successful for your efforts, or that you have come up short, this is the piece of you that sees the results of your actions. It knows that what you put into an endeavor is what you will get out of it, and sometimes that may not be what or as much as you expect. Or maybe it's more. It is though, a direct result of the energy you put towards it, whatever it ends up being.

TEN OF PENTACLES

A big goal in life is to be comfortable and content. When you have what you need, you can relax. You are not in survival mode trying to get this, or get that in order to feel secure. You have it already. Now you can focus on enjoying it. It's not a matter of having more money in the bank than you know what to do with, but about comfortably having what you need. It's about comfortably having what you need for yourself, and having enough to provide for others that you care about. To provide others with what they need is to form a strong union. It is to create a foundation of familial harmony in which each member of the family feels safe and provided for. This piece of you that recognizes yourself as part of a unit of security and gratification is the Ten of Pentacles.

Imagine that you live on a farm and it is harvest time. For months, you have worked in the fields, toiling to make sure your crops are doing fine. You have spent hours weeding them, keeping bugs off them, watering them, and keeping pests away that would harm them. The conditions remained right throughout the season, just enough rain, enough sunny days, and minimal botherations from animals and insects. You have done well to create this bounty, and it is time to enjoy it.

Is this all for you though? Did you do all this work just to consume the entire harvest by yourself? You have a lot. You have plenty to share. There are others who will appreciate it. You want to see them happy and provided for. Of course you're going to share. This was the plan all along. Everybody gets to eat. Everybody gets to be fed and to be nourished. This has come about as a result of your efforts, and you can bask in the good feelings that gives you. This is the Ten of Pentacles within you at its full glory.

The simple knowing that others have what they need is the reward that your Ten of Pentacles receives. It does not seek anything in return except for simple appreciation, and a little of that goes a long ways. A little appreciation will fuel this piece of you to keep on doing what it does. A lot of appreciation will be appreciated too, but just a little is enough. Life being what it is though, sometimes that appreciation does not come its way. This doesn't change anything. The Ten of Pentacles in you still wants what's best for others, and will continue to provide it. It will just do it for the sake of knowing the difference that needs to be made is made, and that nobody they care about is going to falter, fall or go hungry. Deep inside the heart of your inner Ten of Pentacles, that matters way more than accolades.

Contentment, peace of mind, and security are best enjoyed shared with loved ones. This is what drives your inner Ten of Pentacles. It is what keeps it going and makes it happy. When others are happy, so is it. And it likes to be happy, so it will always strive to see others cared for.

PAGE OF PENTACLES

Your Page of Pentacles is your inner child, calculating and innovative. It sees the end results of the goals it wants to achieve, and sets out to achieve them. It doesn't always know how it will come about, just that it must. It knows perfectly well, without ambiguity, what the accumulation of its efforts are going to be, and anything that differentiates from that precisely defined goal is unacceptable. The thing is though, it may not know exactly what all the steps or procedures are to make it happen. It has questions to ask. It has experiments to try. It has routines to figure out to perfect its processes. Your inner Page of Pentacles knows what it wants and will do what it takes to get it.

This is the piece of you that doesn't have all the answers, and is not ashamed in the least to admit that. It knows that in order to get what it wants, it needs to learn many things, and it will learn these things fearlessly and without hesitating to ask people who know the answers, and to follow anybody who might be going where they want to be. This is the best way for it to learn. Some like to figure thing out on their own and take pride in what they learn that way, but not your inner Page of Pentacles. Figuring things out on its own is a pure waste of time when it can go straight to sources of wisdom and knowledge.

Indulge your inner Page of Pentacles by exploring processes. Discover what makes things work. Figure out the causes of various happenings. Make educated guesses and see how close to right you are about them. This piece of you wants to know how the world works and what makes people tick. Help it discover that. Observe the processes of life. Be a people watcher. Make note of what happens when you do such and such a thing. Does this same thing happen every time you do this thing? Are there variations to the result? Your inner Page of Pentacles wants to know, so be as observant as possible and remember what you see. This will help it to grow and to expand its awareness of the world. This is important to your inner Page of Pentacles.

As a communicator, your inner Page of Pentacles doesn't have time for superfluous talk, it wants to get down to business. When it has questions, it wants answers. It doesn't want a lot of extra words to sift through to figure out what is important. There is no time for that. It just wants to get to the point. Small talk and joking around is annoying. This piece of you has scant use for that sort of thing and often despises being subjected to it.

Your inner Page of Pentacles is a practical Fool. While the Fool loves the process of discovery, setting off on an unchartered journey to see where he ends up, the Page of Pentacles is too uncomfortable with such uncertainty. Although this piece of you appreciates the journey, it wants to know where it is going, how it will get there, and what to expect along the way. It will map the route out ahead of time with the exact GPS coordinates. This piece of you is sensible to a fault and does not like surprises.

KNIGHT OF PENTACLES

The Knight of Pentacles within you knows that to be successful, you need to take chances. You need to gamble. You need to throw caution to the wind and hope for the best. It is normal to count on luck. But what is luck exactly? Luck is the aligning of hope and circumstances. You can't always just sit there and wait for luck to show up. You need to prompt it. You need to create the circumstances that foster the possibility of a favorable outcome. If you never try, there is no reason to expect much. You need to try and hope for the best. Trying takes courage, sometimes. So find the courage. It takes faith to try sometimes. So find the faith. Don't let arbitrary winds decide your fate. Take chances, because if you never try, you will never succeed. Don't be afraid to go for it. You can't win what you never risk. So don't fear risks. The Knight of Pentacles embraces the chance to take some risks for the opportunity to prove its self.

The Knight of Pentacles is a confident piece of you. It knows that it has the power to succeed. It also knows that if it does not succeed the first time, then it needs to try again. Success sometimes comes following a succession of failures, so does it make sense to give up after the first? Every failure is an invitation to examine what you have done and see what you could have done differently for a better outcome. Somewhere in that is what you did wrong, and once you figure that out, you get a clue as to what to do right next time. Do this enough times, and eventually you will get it right.

The Knight of Pentacles has little use for negative influences. It knows itself well enough to not be affected by attempts to bring it down. This piece of you asks, "Why listen to naysayers?" It listens to the voice within that says

"Yes I can" and not the voices outside that say "No you can't."

This piece of you needs to be careful. It can get a little cocky and overly sure of itself. It can be so sure that it has the best ideas and the best answers, and it will drag other people into its pipe dreams with promises of great things with no absolute sure way to fulfill those promises. This can drive other people crazy. This can push people away. Not every gamble is going to pay off. When it is just you involved in a bad gamble, that is one thing. You can figure out how to bounce back from it and stabilize. When you drag other people into your unrealistic expectations and deplete their material and emotional resources, you have done them a disservice, and they will remember this about you. It is your reputation that takes a hit, so be careful.

As a communicator, the Knight of Pentacles within you is charming and persuasive. It has mastered the art of the sales pitch and can put a positive spin on just about everything. It knows what it wants, and how you fit into the scheme of things. With this, it knows what to say to get what it wants from you. It is a smooth talker.

Your inner Knight of Pentacles can at times be stubborn. This is because it wants what it wants and has little patience and tolerance for anybody who is in its way of getting it. In its quest for perfection, it may make people feel unappreciated and pushed aside. It doesn't mean to hurt anybody's feelings though, and will probably apologize for any such offenses. A tunnel vision approach to achieving its goals is the best way it knows.

QUEEN OF PENTACLES

Your inner Queen of Pentacles is very much a people person. She is intuitive and able to read the needs of others. Once she senses the needs of others, she cannot ignore them. She takes them on as her own needs and seeks to provide. She cannot walk away or turn her back on anybody she can help. Her heart is is bountiful and easily opened to those who need her. She cannot help but to care, and wants to provide materially so that there is no sense of lack in the lives of those she loves. She will feel best about her success if she can share it with others.

The Queen of Pentacles is tuned in. The feelings, needs, and emotions of those around her are constantly soaking into her through energetic osmosis. As she feels what others feel, she reacts to them. If there is problem, she wants to solve it for them. If there is joy, she wants to share it. If there is fear, she wants to placate it. If there is conflict, she wants to resolve it. If there is doubt, she will find surety. She is empathic and very aware. Wanting to help is just who she is.

The Queen of Pentacles is essentially the Empress tending to her garden. While she is not actively at this moment planting new seeds, she is taking care of what has blossomed. What needs do they have? How can she help? If she senses distress, what is the root cause of it, and what can she do to resolve it? Intuition will guide her to these answers.

This piece of you needs to me mindful not to be overbearing. With as much as she loves others and wants to maintain a healthy overall sense of being for them, she needs to understand that sometimes the best thing is to let people figure these things out on their own. The Queen of Pentacles cannot always solve other people's problems no matter how badly she wants to. She has to accept that for the sake of their growth, sometimes people need to solve their own problems. These people are not there to be spoiled by your Queen of Pentacles. Spoiling them and giving them an easy way out is not always the best approach. Sometimes this piece of you needs to step back and give space to these people.

As a communicator, your inner Queen of Pentacles is inquisitive. She likes to know what others are thinking and what they need. She may probe to find an understanding of how she can be of service. She is not being nosey, even if she seems like she is. She just cares. If she has to be intrusive to figure out how to be helpful, that's what she's going to do.

Your inner Queen of Pentacles often puts the needs of others ahead of her own. Her satisfaction comes from knowing that these other people are cared for and are having their needs met. This brings the satisfaction that she herself needs.

KING OF PENTACLES

The King of Pentacles is that piece of you that can generate much from very little. This piece of you can go from a humble start, to amassing something significant and profound. Others may look on in awe and wonder how you did it. And you may wonder yourself, how exactly did I do this? You did it through a keen business sense, an entrepreneurial spirit, intuition, and a sharp mind.

It takes more than luck to amass a fortune. It takes skills and know how as well. It also takes patience and courage. Fortunes seldom pop up over night. It is the result of a well planned plan, and the acceptance that the plan is a stepping stone process. It is not generally a singular event that is the Big Bang event of your fortune, but a series of sometimes significant, often mundane steps.

As you achieve one small part of the overall goal, you create the platform for the next step. You move on to achieve that, and you create the platform for the next, and the next. You keep creating these stepping stones until you reach the destination that is represented by the goal of success you have set for yourself. You manifest your goals through the patience it takes for each stepping stone to become reality. Don't let impatience slow you down. Rushing ahead is seldom wise. Letting things take the time they need to come into being is the path to achievement.

The King of Pentacles is goal oriented and a good strategist. He can envision the outcomes of his gambles and actions and make his moves accordingly. He is shrewd and unafraid to make a power play when he needs to. He knows what he wants and will make the move to get it, even if he has to step on people in the process.

He is proud of his achievements. He likes to reflect on his moves that got him where he is in life. He can be a mentor and help others achieve their own success as well. He gets his way and creates his success through force and determination. He will scan both his competition as well as anybody who is in his way to ascertain their weaknesses so that he can exploit them in his quest for his own success. He also ascertains their strengths so as not to be taken by surprise by their power plays. He is able to anticipate their moves and has a number of contingency plans in place to react to them. He likes to win.

The King of Pentacles' communication style is suave and charming. His mission is more than the simple communication of facts and pleasantries, he often delves into your psyche. If he is trying to sell you something, he is looking for a hook. If he views you as competition, he may be looking for something to use against you, maybe now, maybe later. If he is hoping to make allies, he could be looking for common ground. With the King of Pentacles, communication often has ulterior motives.

The King of Pentacles within you is that piece of yourself that is not afraid of success. And why should it be? What good does it do any of us to not live the fullest and strongest version of ourselves? How are we doing ourselves any good by not doing what we know we can do to be successful? The King of Pentacles doesn't hold back. He goes full force on his power. He gets past his limiting beliefs that tell him to slow down, that others won't handle his success very well, and laughs at the idea of not living up to his greatest potential. He doesn't let past mistakes and frustrations keep him from trying again, and again, and again for as many times as it takes to get it right. He aims high and sets a course for success.

Part Four: Wands

The pieces of ourselves related to our passions

ACE OF WANDS

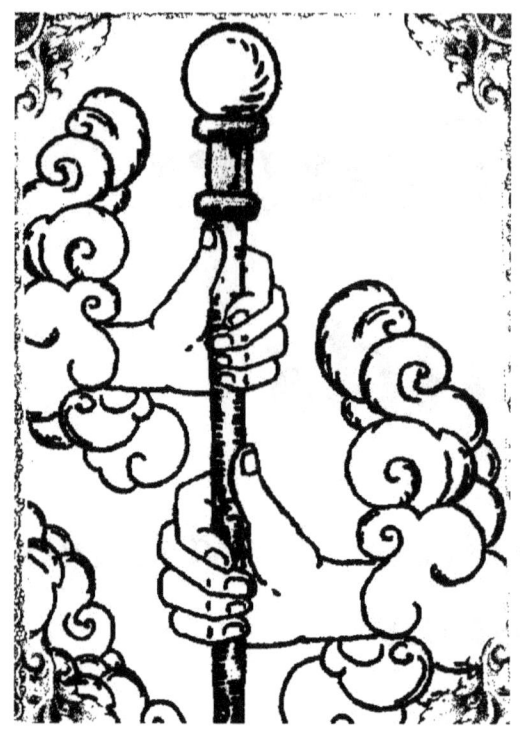

The Ace of Wands within you is a spark. This is the spark of your passion, and it has been ignited. You have discovered something new that excites you, and you want to explore all aspects of it. You want to master it. You want to create a paradigm in which this new passion is paramount. So do it. Focus your attention on this passion. Coax that spark into a fire. Let it become an inferno. Be all you can be in the context of this new passion. Make it your life. Keep the fire roaring by your devotion to it. The raw material is there to be great. Don't ignore it. Use it to become a master and an inspiration as you become as great as you can be. Don't settle for less. Go big.

Your Ace of Wands is a sudden burst of energy towards an ambition and a goal. Maybe there is something you have been thinking about doing. Maybe you've had an idea to write a book, or to do some woodworking projects, or something like that. You're thinking about it, but you just, as of yet, have not had that surge of inspiration to really kick it into gear. The Ace of Wands is that surge. It is the inspiration and the energy to kick off your endeavor. You will find it, you just need to be open to it and be willing to act on it. When it hits you, jump on it. Don't say, "Yeah. That's a good idea. I'll do it tomorrow." Do it today. Tomorrow will take the rawness from it and wilt its power. Jump on the inspiration while it is still hot.

Once inspiration cools down, you may or not be able to get it hot again. So as soon as it hits you, do something with it. You can't always predict where inspiration will come from, so you never know if you can make your way back to it if you don't seize it when it comes to you. Inspiration is a seed that if properly nourished, will grow into something fruitful and abundant. When inspired, realize there is something that is ready to be manifest on the earth, and through you, this manifestation will happen. Don't lose the opportunity to be the manifestation agent because you let it slip away.

Your inner Ace of Wands is telling you to not wait for permission to come into your power and talents. You know what are capable of. You know what you can do, so don't hold back waiting for somebody external to yourself to give you the go ahead. Like, maybe you are a gifted writer, but you are not yet comfortable writing brilliantly, until somebody tells you that you should work at it. Maybe you are afraid that important people in your life will be disappointed that you are pursuing this instead of something else, or that they will be jealous that you have this talent and they don't. So you deliberately hold back on shining as brightly as you can on purpose.

Once you know that these people in your life support you and appreciate what you are able to do though, then you are more comfortable with your talents. Now you feel like you have permission to shine your own light. The trick to living fully is to learn how to not wait for this permission, to identify within yourself these shining lights of personal power and talent. Remind yourself to shine them as brightly as possible no matter what fear you have of what others may think or of what jealousies you may inspire. This is your life. You have the right to live it the best you can.

Just because you aren't dead doesn't mean you're living. If you are not living your passion, then are you really alive? There is more to being alive than just being alive. Being alive means being so with a purpose, however lofty or mundane that may be. When you go after purpose, you are alive with your passion. This is what life is really about. Your inner Ace of Wands is always there to help you shine.

TWO OF WANDS

Inspiration is great.
But do you know what is even better? Acting on it! The Two of Wands within you knows this. This is the piece of you that becomes the driving force that gets things done. This is the piece of you that tugs at you and nags you to get busy. It urges you to not procrastinate. It is that sense of incompleteness that you feel until you develop a plan of attack towards achieving whatever that inspiration is that you feel. This is the piece of you that waters and nurtures that seed of inspiration that is the Ace of Wands.

After being inspired, it is time to make a plan to act on that inspiration. It is time to truly see in the eye of your mind, the final outcome of this inspiration. What exactly does it look like? Visualize it so you will know what it looks like when you accomplish it. How will you know you reached it? How will you know that you did everything you needed to do to achieve the goal put into place by the inspiration? Remember, inspiration is given to us. It seemingly comes from out of nowhere, sometimes. It is an idea, and that is all it is. It is a glimpse of an outcome we can achieve if we put the work in to achieving it, but it's not going to achieve itself. No, achievement is up to you. Devise a plan, and then get busy.

The Two of Wands endeavors to keep you out of ruts. Ruts happen. We become complacent in our lives and think we have all we need. Sure, maybe we are right. Maybe we do have all we need. Maybe we have the food, shelter, companionship, entertainment, and whatever else we consider important to our day to day survival. But is that all it is? Day to day to survival? If you want more, you need to work for it. You need to seize those inspirations that are provided to you and appreciate them as opportunities to take your life and your existence to new levels.

You have so much at your disposal to create the life of your dreams that you can't possibly use all of it. This means that realistically, you want for nothing. This means that the time is nigh to do something great. All you have to do is do it. So do it! To not do it is to severely sell yourself short. Listen to the Two of Wands. It is screaming this at you. If you sell yourself short, you are likewise selling short those who could benefit from your success. So if you are not doing all you can do for your own sake, do it for them. The world is in your hands. Make it matter.

You have talents and skills waiting to be tapped into. Are you tapping into them? Are you waiting for them to be brought to the surface through a need to express them? That's fair enough. Sometimes it will be like that. You don't always know what you can do, until there is no choice but to step up and do them. When this happens, don't back down or shy away. Express this newly discovered side of your self, use the strength it provides, and allow this to integrate into the whole of who you are. This is exciting, so look for these things. Look for these dormant qualities, sleeping in hibernation, just waiting to be awakened and utilized.

It happens that we start to feel stuck and stagnant in situations. We just get lulled into patterns and cycles and we forget that we have the choice to make changes. So when you feel stuck, when you feel like you have achieved all you can achieve and are not meant for more, ask yourself, why? Why do you feel like that? Imagine what it is that that you wish you were doing, as opposed to what it is you are doing, and ask yourself, "Why am I not doing what I want to do? Why have I allowed myself to get stuck in this rut?" And then seek the answer to that question. Once you have the answer, address it. Make a plan. Unstuck yourself! It is your life. Remember that. Live it to the best of your abilities by following your dreams, passions and bliss. You have the whole world in your hands. Make your life what you want it to be.

THREE OF WANDS

You have been inspired. You have a vision of what the actualization of this inspiration looks like. You created a game plan for yourself to achieve this goal, and you have made progress. Now you can see how things are going, what is working and what needs tweaking. You have remained flexible, making allowances for new ideas that can only improve on your original thought. You have a good sense of how it will all come together, and an idea of what else needs to be done to perfect the actualization of your vision. You have put in the work, and you know what else needs to be done. The piece of you that assesses and sees these things is the Three of Wands.

You're doing it. It's happening. You are making progress, but you still wonder if there is anything else you should or could be doing. When this is where you find yourself, imagine a distant horizon. Over there, your dream waits for you. It's already there. It's already real. You just need to get to it. The Three of Wands urges you to not just look at that distant horizon, but to create a plan to get there. The first step of realizing your dreams is to dream them. Sound simple? It is. Imagine the realization of your greatest ambitions. Visualize what it means to have it, to live it, to be it. Imagine not just what it is like to go there and to get there, but to be there. Dream of arriving.

Let the dream of arriving, of being there, become so strong that the essence of manifestation cannot be denied. Let the essence of manifestation become so strong that it cannot help but to become reality. This is how dreams become real. So, dream. You know what you want. Don't give the universe a choice but to give it to you.

Dream of the lands where you would like to arrive. Dream of them so big that they fill you until you cannot contain them within the confines of you anymore. Let them spill into reality. Let all you dream of, hope for, crave, desire become so intense that they can stay inside the framework of your imagination no longer. Allow them to spill into the world of reality. This is what it means to dream so big that that the dream has no choice but to become real. Let your dream, by default, become manifest.

It is a big world and there is much to do, see, and experience. Take note of where your dreams, inspirations, and thoughts take you, for they will take you to many territories that have yet to be explored. Why not go to them? You can go literally. You can see what is beyond your normal scope of vision by traveling to them and seeing them and living them first hand. Or it can be done figuratively. Learn something new. Take a class. Find a new blog to read. Get a library card, and then use it. Fill your awareness with new and different influences. Experience new ideas and new thoughts about the meaning of life. There is a lot out there. The Three of Wands encourages you to go forth and experience every horizon you can possibly dream of.

FOUR OF WANDS

You did it. After being inspired and working hard to achieve your visions, you have finally reached a point where you feel a sense of achievement. You accomplished what you set out to accomplish, and maybe you accomplished even more. Congratulate yourself. You have done a good job. And you know what else? Your accomplishments have not gone unnoticed by other people. They see what you have done, and they are impressed. You have come a long way from where you started. The Four of Wands within you is there to acknowledge you. It sees what you have done, and it knows that other people see it too. It is the piece of you that wants you to know you have done a good job.

Validation can be a powerful motivator. To know that what you have done is appreciated by others, aren't you more in the mood to do more? It feels good to know that what you have done has a positive impact on others. This takes the inspiration you had, and the goals and dreams you worked for to its ultimate conclusion. These things that you have spent so much of your time and energy on where not merely for your sole benefit, but for the good of others as well. Having accomplished your vision for their behalf, they are now saying thank you. Feel good about that.

The Four of Wands reminds you to celebrate. Celebrate your hard work. Celebrate the hard work of others. Appreciate one another's dreams, visions, goals and realities. Good things are given to those who work hard for them. Notice this. See what you have created, and see what others have created too. Be there to express appreciation. Let people know that their dreams were not accomplished in a vacuum, that their reach goes beyond the confines of their own awareness; you feel them too. By letting them know this, they will be inspired to do more, create more, dream more, reach for more, and accomplish more.

Accomplishing your dreams creates a domino affect. Doesn't it? Once you do one thing, don't you put your mind to what you can do next? What other dreams you can tackle, since you know you are completely capable of making things happen? This is what it means to be a creator, and we all have it in us to create. Dreams build on dreams. Once your dream is realized, go for more. Make it bigger. Make your dream an empire. A dream doesn't have to be a one shot deal. No, it can multiply and expand. It can spin off into other dreams, each of which can spin off into even more.

Acknowledgement of your accomplishments, whether it is privately or publicly by others is a way to finalize them. Recognition makes them official. Now you can say "I did it." Whatever your dreams were, recognize the effort and energy that went into making them reality. This makes it appealing to keep going and to do more.

FIVE OF WANDS

You don't always know what you can do until you push yourself to do it. You don't always push yourself until you have to prove yourself. You don't always have to prove yourself until you are challenged. You are not always challenged until you have competition that is trying to be better than you. When somebody is trying to be better than you, and you are intent on showing them that they are not, then it is time to step up and really show what you are capable of. You may have to hone some skills and bring yourself up to a new level. In so doing, you are on your way to mastering whatever skill this is. This is the Five of Wands within you. It thrives on this competition. It is that piece of you that has a healthy ego that pushes you to new levels of perfection.

Challenges come up that force you to dig deep within yourself to find resources and hidden skills and talents that you didn't know you had. There could be a talent or a skill that is latent within you. This could be something that you have never had to utilize before, so it is something you are untested at. This does not mean that you are not able to do it, it just means that until now, you have not been called upon to. But once you find that skill within yourself, once you come to an understanding of it, now you can test yourself at it. You can get to understand and master it. Through facing challenges and overcoming obstacles, you become stronger by finding these latent skills and talents, and then putting them to the test.

The Five of Wands is the piece of you that will not let yourself give up.

When a difficulty comes up, or when you are faced with obstacles and challenges, there may be a voice in your head that says, "Give up. It's too hard. What difference does it make, anyway?" This voice can be compelling as you consider just how much effort it really would take to overcome whatever problem this is. The voice may be very convincing as it works to undermine your confidence in your abilities to solve problems. Without the Five of Wands urging you to dig deep and work hard, you may very well listen to that voice and give up. So be thankful for the Five of Wands for urging you to keep fighting and find the solutions and answers. Be glad for the positive dose of ego it injects into you for the sake of being the best version of yourself.

The Five of Wands encourages you to embrace challenges. So many good things come to you through facing challenges. By facing challenges and getting through them, you learn many things about yourself. You discover what you are truly capable of, you get a glimpse of where and how you fit into the grand scheme of things, you gain competence, and you validate your own skills and talents. Never back down from something that is important to you just because it looks difficult. Look at that difficulty and say, "This may look impossible, but it's not. How fortunate I am for the chance to awaken that piece of me that can overcome this." Then find that piece, and wake it up. Shock it to life. Put it to work and get the work done.

Once done, you can say you did it. You will have the satisfaction of not giving up and seeing this thing through to completion. You can be happy that you didn't let somebody else subjugate you to their insistence that they are better than you. You proved that you can stand your ground against this competition. You proved, even if only to yourself, that you are able to do anything at all that you decide you want to do, and nobody or anything has the power to convince you otherwise.

SIX OF WANDS

The Six of Wands is the piece of you that feels validated, and this validation is well deserved. It is not a forced validation brought about by a "poor me" attitude that makes people fawn over you just to make you feel better because you are acting pitiful. No, this is genuine appreciation for what you have done. This is recognition for a job well done and appreciation for the good it does for all. This is not validation that pumps up the ego to unhealthy proportions, but validation that fuels future actions to do more. It is general human nature for a person to do more for people when they know that what they are doing is noticed and valued. The Six of Wands is the piece of you that attracts this notice.

Give credit where credit is due. When you see that somebody has done a good job, tell them. Let them know, but make sure it is sincere. If it is not sincere, it is pointless. When it is sincere and deserved, don't hold back. Give praise. This lets people know that their energy was not for nothing. This creates a synergy as your gratitude for them is received and reflected back to you with their appreciation for having been witnessed in a positive way. Think about it. Don't you like genuine appreciation? Can't you detect false flattery?

How about yourself, are you giving yourself enough credit? Even if you are, give yourself a little more. You deserve it. Others know this. They may shower you with accolades and praise, but do you give your own self a pat on the back? Do you celebrate your accomplishments and the milestones you reach in life? Take a moment to do this. Reflect on the journey that got you to where you are right now with an emphasis on the positive. If you are worried that doing this makes you seem full of yourself or egotistical to others, then do it quietly. Run through an inventory of your achievements in your mind and have your own private celebration.

Imagine yourself a hero returning home. Imagine that in pursuit of your goal, you went away to work on achieving it. Imagine that in doing this, you had battles to fight. So you fought them. You fought them and you won. By winning, you achieved what you set out to achieve, and now your goals are met. These goals are for your own betterment, as well as the betterment of those you care about. Having accomplished this, now you can return home.
You have returned, changed for the better. You have returned with an expanded world view, more refined talents, and a renewed sense of purpose. What does this mean exactly? You have had the opportunity to refine your skills and abilities. You have gone within and found resources and strength that you can now apply to most any circumstance. You truly have the chance to show others exactly what these are.

There are those who have long waited for your return, and now they get to see just how you have grown, how you have changed. The star quality that they remember about you has grown and now shines brighter. It will bring you much happiness to express this part of yourself again, and it will give those who admire you a thrill to witness it again. The Six of Wands wants you to know that you have done a good job and it encourages you to tap into your personal power and do more.

SEVEN OF WANDS

When a seemingly insurmountable obstacle comes your way that stops you in your tracks, and you say, "I can't go any farther." The Seven of Wands within you says, "Yes you can. You just need to find a different way." Listen to these words of wisdom. Take them to heart, then, find that different way. Don't let obstacles stop you. Keep going.

You know what you want. You have a vision of what you are going to accomplish. You see in your mind's eye what it looks like to accomplish what you are working to accomplish. It's not as easy as you thought it would be though. Problems come up. Obstacles arise. Blocks roll in front of your path to accomplishments. What do you do when these things happen? You know your pursuits are worth your while to work for, but you are just not completely sure how to bring them to actuality.

When that happens, the first thing to do is not give up. Consider it a challenge, and challenges are not meant to make you doubt yourself or your abilities. They are there to prompt you to go beyond your limitations to see things you have not previously seen. They are there to expand your peripheral vision to see what is on the fringes. If the solution is not immediately in front of you, then it is elsewhere. You know it's there somewhere, right? Keep looking for it.

Solutions aren't always obvious. They often require creative thinking. So get creative. Be ridiculously creative. Be so creative that people think you are crazy. This may very well be what it takes to get past the obstacles that have come up. "This is so crazy it just might work." Remember that cliche, because it is a good one. Prove yourself to be a mad genius. This can be fun. Let people wonder what you are up to and try to figure you out. When you find that the solutions are outside the realm of conventionality, you may inspire them to go beyond their own comfort zones in the quest for the solutions they are looking for. It can take a dose of insanity to do that, so be insane. You're allowed.

The Seven of Wands encourages you to be detail oriented. You have to be when you are trying to figure something out. You need to examine everything to see what contributes to the solution, and what is superfluous. When taking innovative and unique approaches to problem solving, you have a lot of ideas to sift through. You have a lot of trial and error to work out. By paying attention the first time to what works and what doesn't work, you save yourself a lot of trouble and time by not having to repeat the same mistakes.

Think of it as walking through a giant maze. How many times do you want to keep hitting the same wall? It would be so much nicer to remember your steps and avoid the barriers you already hit. Take new steps. Explore other corridors. Go ways you haven't tried yet, because you know one of those ways is the way you are looking for, not the ones you already tried that turned out to be wrong.

When solution hunting, don't let your past frustrations become obstacles. This happens. We remember a complication or a negative outcome to something we once tried to do, and assume it will be the same if we try again. So we resist trying again. Our mind is already made up as to what the outcome will be.

The trick is to convince yourself that this new occurrence of the situation is a second chance. Consider what went wrong, or what you didn't do right last time, and do it a different way this time. Visualize a positive outcome. Imagine what went wrong, and see it going right this time. In this way, you dissolve the obstacles in front of you and make your way past them as if they were never there to begin with. If you are going to be greater than you already are in life, this is a necessary skill to get the hang of.

Your inner Seven of Wands wants you to achieve your greatest and highest good. It wants you to aim high and achieve beyond your best potential. It knows though, that this is a lofty goal, but not impossible. By applying your best efforts and by not giving up when things get tough, you will make this happen.

EIGHT OF WANDS

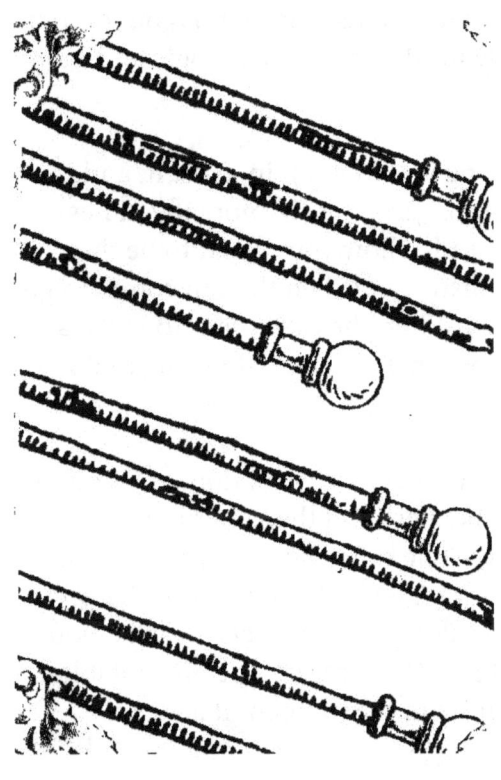

You need to act fast sometimes. Opportunities come up, and if you don't do something with them quickly, you are going to lose them, and it won't be anybody's fault but your own. Do you want that to happen? Do you want to live with the regret that you lost out on something important, or at the very least, something really cool because you hesitated or were lazy? It's all up to you. When a door opens, step through it before it closes. When a window opens, stick your head through it and see what you have at your disposal before it slams shut again. Take advantage of the situation. If you don't, you're the one who will miss out. The Eight of Wands within you will point these opportunities out to you. Don't squander them.

There are going to be those times in life when you need to think fast. You don't always have time to go slow and think things through. Make a quick assessment of the situation and make up your mind. When you don't have time to consider all aspects of whatever the situation is, then your intuition is paramount. What is your gut telling you? This may be all you have to go on, so learn to listen to it and learn to trust it. Hope that you make the right decision, but if you feel like you didn't, how can you work with what you ended up with? Find the best of the situation and adjust to the paradigm of it. If you can't change it, what else can you do? There is no point beating yourself over it. You did the best you could with the time you had to do it. This is just how life is.

Sometimes we tell ourselves we will do such and such thing "When the time is right." So we wait and wait and wait for this magic moment when the time is right. Maybe we say, "We'll have children when the time is right." Or, "I'll sell my house when the time is right." Things like that. But what does that really mean? What does it mean to be "right?" We spend so much time waiting for these ambiguous moments that we miss out on pure opportunities that arise. Sometimes we need to rely less on logic and more on intuition and go for it.

Listen to your gut. It is wise. If it is telling you to jump in, trust it, and jump. The conditions may not be right for jumping anymore if you hesitate too long. So let your gut take the lead. Allow your mind to be the follower, and don't second guess your instincts. When the call comes to go, go. When the call comes to jump, jump. When the call comes to make a change, make the change. You will know when it's the right thing to do, so don't question it.

The Eight of Wands within you is there to make sure you don't miss out. It will tell you that you may make a mistake here and there, but it urges you to not live in fear of those mistakes. Don't be so fearful that you will mess up that you never try. Go for what you want when the opportunities present themselves to do so. You will have much greater regrets for what you missed out on than for what you went for. These regrets are preventable. All you have to do is do it, whatever "it" is in the moment it arises.

NINE OF WANDS

Success isn't always easy to achieve. Neither is peace of mind. Sometimes no matter what we do to achieve and hold onto these things, it is never enough. No matter what we do, it feels like somebody or something punches us in the gut, knocks us down, and keeps us from ever getting what we want. They are constantly throwing obstacles in front of us and it seems like that we can't possibly get ahead. Sometimes it is true. But we can't let that keep us from going for what we want. What we want is ours to have no matter what is in our way of getting it. We need to roll with these punches, and never give up. We are meant for success, and peace of mind is never too much to ask for.

The Nine of Wands within you is like a boxing trainer in your corner of the ring. Think about Micky in the movie Rocky, encouraging you to get up and keep fighting when you get knocked down. This piece of you sees the best in you. It sees the heart that you have, and it pushes you to keep going no matter how desperate things may seem. You have personal power, and the Nine of Wands knows what that power is. This power has nothing to do with letting life's challenges crush you, but everything to do with rolling with the punches that get thrown at you in the course of just being yourself. The Nine of Wands recognizes when you are in pain, and it wants you to know that all is never lost. It will remind you that behind the clouds, the sun is still shining, and those clouds won't be there forever. It will remind you that bruises heal. Cuts and scrapes get better. In darkness, there is always a spark of light, and if you focus on that spark of light, it will grow greater and greater. It will become brighter and brighter. In time, it will overtake the darkness, and your life will shine once again.

The Nine of Wands reminds you to set a beacon of what contentment is to you, and stay focused on your own idea about how life should be lived. Stick to what your own ideas of what happiness is, and live this way no matter what. When you get knocked off course, find that beacon and drift towards it again. It will remind you to handle a little criticism and not let anything bother you just because it is not what you want to hear. Maintain a strong sense of self and do not let it bother you when you and others don't see eye to eye. When you fall down, get back up. Where others may shrink, find the fertilizer to grow.

It is important to not take everything personally. Others may attack you and endeavor to keep you in your place, but the Nine of Wands is within you to remind you that this is reflective of problems and attitudes that these people have. It's not about you. It is unfortunate that you have to bear the brunt of their negative world view, but you can't always change people; not everybody is open to be changed. Sometimes negative people are just negative people. If they are unhappy with something about themselves, sometimes they lash out at who or whatever is convenient. Sometimes, that may be you. Develop the strength to not be knocked down by them, and if you do get knocked down, don't stay down. Get back up and keep living your life.

The Nine of Wands is that piece of you that is not a quitter. It doesn't give up and it doesn't let things bother it unnecessarily. It is the piece of you that knows what joy means, and will find its way back to it when it is knocked away from it. This is the piece of you that maintains its true sense of self.

TEN OF WANDS

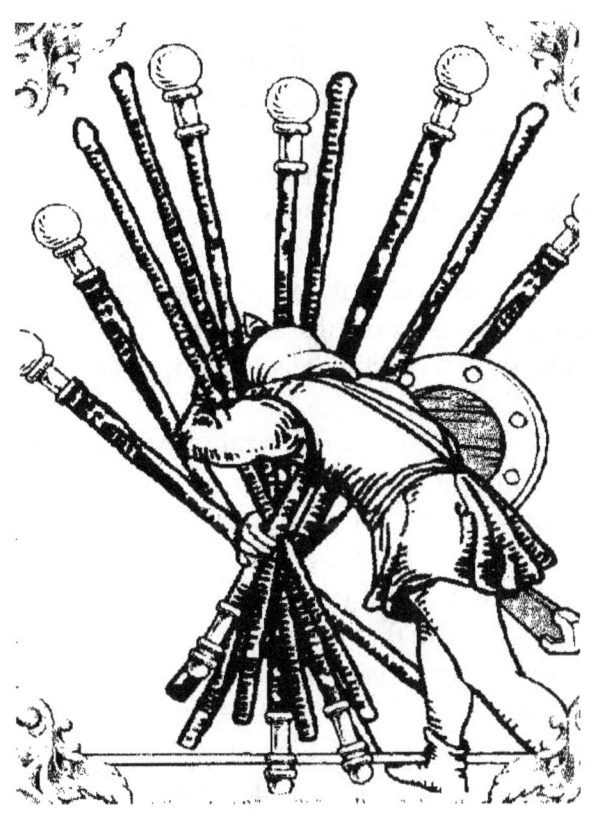

The Ten of Wands is the piece of you that keeps up with all that you are. It keeps track of your many talents and skills. There may be one dominate talent or skill that you most identify with. Perhaps you are a brilliant piano player, and this is how you define yourself, as a brilliant piano player. But is playing the piano all you do? Is "piano player" the only thing you identify as? You may be a piano player, but maybe you're also a soccer coach. Maybe you are a piano playing soccer coach who is also a woodworker. This is what it means to be multitalented and multifaceted. Just because you have one talent or skill set, doesn't mean that you don't have others as well. Are you getting personal satisfaction from the balance of all you do?

Often times, we work hard to achieve something important in our life, and we achieve it. This gives us personal satisfaction and we feel good about it. It does though, create responsibilities. What we created, we must now work to maintain. We must keep up with it. We can't let our creation crumble or fall apart. This takes commitment and energy. We may discover that it is taking more than we had bargained for. As we work to keep up with this one thing, other things are occurring to us too. Our other talents and skill sets want to be recognized and utilized. At this point, we must consider what is the most important. It may be time to delegate. This thing that you have created, can you trust it with somebody else as you pursue another passion? Could it be it is time to put it to rest for the sake of what is new? Can it coast on autopilot as you put your time and energy towards this new endeavor?

The average person has more than one thing on their mind at any given time. Likewise, they are involved in more than one pursuit. Few are singularly focused to the point that they tune out 100% of other things in favor of only one specific point of attention. Even an obstetrician delivering twins might be thinking about what's for dinner that night. That's human nature. We let our minds wander and to be engaged in a number of thoughts, problems to be solved, ideas, dreams, hopes, desires, to be achieved, and fears to be overcome. There are any number of things that we are prone to having on our mind in the course of living our lives hour by hour, minute by minute. Humans are complex beings, and this is just how we are. The Ten of Wands within us does its best to keep up with it all.

The question becomes can we multitask? Can we prioritize? Can we accurately decide what is the most important thing to focus on? When we have a lot happening at once, it is easy to let it overwhelm us. The Ten of Wands says though, "Don't let that happen." It advises us to do a lightning fast assessment of all the elements before us, and figure out quickly what is the most important. What is the one thing that if we don't take care of immediately, will cause us distress right now in the moment, and on down the line as well? Make this priority number one. What, if we hold off on it, if we put it on the back burner for later, won't be that big of a deal? The Ten of Wands wants us to keep up with all we need to keep up with, but at the same time not feel an inordinate amount of pressure from it.

The Ten of Wands is that piece of you that wants you to be proud of what you have accomplished, what you are capable of, and who you are. It shows you all you can do, all you have done, and all that life is offering you. It wants you to enjoy these things, but not to be overwhelmed by what obligations they may create. Your talents and skills, the entire multitude of them are meant to enhance your life and to positively effect the lives of others, not to put more on your shoulders than you are meant to carry. The Ten of Wands within you wants you to remember that.

PAGE OF WANDS

The Page of Wands within you wants you to detach from filters. Remove self-doubt. Quiet your inner critic. Now create. It begs you to think back to a time when you had no idea what you couldn't do, so you just did. You did it all. Your imagination was your ultimate guide, and it was unlimited. Put yourself back in that time and do something. Do the things that you could only do when you didn't know you had limits. When you put yourself back in a time and space where you didn't have limits, are you not unlimited? Don't tell yourself you can't do this or that. Just do it. Be creative without boundaries.

Do not lose that part of yourself that wants to explore, or that part of yourself that wants to express yourself in new and different ways. This is that part of yourself that believes itself to be a genius whether it has been tested and proven or not. This is the part of yourself that is not concerned with what others think and will not listen to voices of negativity. It is the part of yourself that still believes that anything can happen, and can tap into unlimited inspiration to create art and creative expressions, as well as innovative solutions to problems in the real world.

The Page of Wands is the piece of yourself that still wants to have fun. It does not want to get so lost in the world of obligations and commitments, and grown up pursuits that it forgets what is important. What is important is what enriches the soul. Having fun is very enriching. Even in situations where grown up activities have to happen, this piece of yourself wants you to remember to smile through it. Find a way to make it fun. Don't become such an adult that child-like fantasy and fun get lost.

Your inner Page of Wands is the inner child of yourself that finds the fire to propel you out of stressful and unhappy situations. It is the piece that can easily be lost and forgotten in adult life, but it is also the piece of you that screams to you when it knows it can help, but you just aren't listening. It has ideas and innovations that can get you through anything. When you get so caught up in the details of stressful living, it will have ideas for you that will help you get through it with a smile on your face.

As a communicator, your inner Page of Wands is optimistic and cheerful. It wants you to stay upbeat. It wants you to see the positive in every situation, and it will communicate in such a way that does not make things worse than they have to be. It is realistic. As much as it wants to look at the world through rose colored glasses, it knows that things aren't always so rosy. But that doesn't mean it's going to sink to the level of any kind of misery that is there. No, it will find the good and hope for the best. It won't add to your worries, but rather try to relieve you of as much of them as it can. It genuinely cares.

The Page of Wands is essentially an optimistic Fool. It doesn't settle for depression or bad feelings. It will fight its way out of these situations with its own passion for living. It will find the light at the end of any tunnel no matter how impenetrable the darkness may seem. It does this with its sense of humor, sense of happiness, and realization that the most important thing in life is to feel happy. It will seek out those things and embrace that which brings joy, not just for itself, but for those it cares about as well.

KNIGHT OF WANDS

Your inner Knight of Wands may take the attitude that sometimes you have to go for broke just to force understanding and a sense of clarity. You have to push yourself over an edge to see if others are going to follow you or not. How do you know where you stand and how do you know where others stand in relation to you if you don't? You really need to push some boundaries sometimes just to see where you are. This can be a do or die proposition as it creates a paradigm where things may or may not be the same for you afterward. You won't know the outcome of it until it is done. You cannot know with certainty how it will play out. It may turn out as you like it to be, or it may not. It can be risky, but a risk you need to take in order to move forward with your life. All you can do is hope for the best as you force this new chapter of your life to begin.

Your inner Knight of Wands knows how to blast through obstacles. What's been slowing you down? Stopping you? Have you been staring at this wall in front of you so long now that you finally see its weak points and fractures? Let the power of your creativity blast this wall down. Tap into your creative resources and get past it in any unique and innovative way that you can. Maybe the solutions you been searching for have been too lofty and complex. Maybe the solution has been simple all this time. Whatever the case may be, the Knight of Wands knows the answer. It has studied it long enough. The time is now to destroy that block and move forward harmoniously. Just simply do it.

The Knight of Wands doesn't look for reasons why something can't be done. He doesn't make excuses. He takes pride in accomplishing what sets out to accomplish, and the more impossible it is, the better. To the Knight of Wands, impossible is not a limitation, it is a challenge. It is a chance to prove its creative skills and its problem solving abilities. Impossible to him, is just a label, and labels are how others define a a situation. They are not intrinsic. They are nothing more than a way for people to categorize and be comfortable with the various entities encountered in life. They are not, however, anything that the Knight of Wands is willing to settle for.

The Knight of Wands likes to rally people. This is how he communicates. He likes to get people together to have some fun, or to get something done. He speaks with confidence and authority to get everybody on his side to convince them to see things his way and to do the things he wants them to do. He likes to be a leader and to provide opportunities for everybody to get together for good times.

Your inner Knight of Wands is not afraid to take chances, because chances are what lead to success. Without chances, no new ground is ever gained, and as a Knight, he is not willing to remain stagnant. Forward momentum is important to him. Chances and risks are what propels him to bigger and better things in life. The chances he takes may or may not pay off exactly as he predicts, but that doesn't bother him. He will roll with the punches and go with the flow. The most important thing to him is, is to not live in fear or worry.

QUEEN OF WANDS

Your inner Queen of Wands is memorable. This is the piece of you that does things that are hard to forget. This is the piece of you that gets noticed for its positive qualities and ability to really make a difference. This piece of you is highly creative, and a master of whatever given skill or talent is your dominate quality. The Queen of Wands guides you to use this skill or talent to be of use in this world. You know you are respected and admired for this, but you don't let it go to your head. It makes you happy to do these things, and this is what motivates you. The fact that others look up to you for doing it is just a nice bonus.

The Queen of Wands takes the common and does something uncommon with it. This is what it means to be a writer, to be an artist, to be the master of any talent. Your inner Queen of Wands takes the mundane and makes it memorable. She takes the forgettable and makes it spectacular. She takes the predictable and twists it out of shape until it is something nobody expected it would ever be. This is what being a creative genius is about. A creative genius is not bound by conventionality. A creative genius sees what others do not, and expresses it in a way that is understandable.

The Queen of Wands within you is that creative powerhouse. She is an unstoppable force that has one creative impulse after another. These impulses are not passive things to her. They are not things to be looked at, considered, and ultimately dismissed. They are divine forces waiting to be realized, and she is more than happy to be the one to realize them. Through her, inspiration takes shape and form on the earth. Through her, they are more than simple thoughts. They are purposes to be realized.

The Queen of Wands has the ability to create and to be an influence. She encourages you to get out of your head and do what you know you can do. She makes you make it happen. She is rich and abundant with ideas. She plants these ideas in your awareness to be given birth to. So do it. Give birth to these ideas. The gestation period is complete. They are ready for the world. The sooner you do it, the sooner the world will benefit from your brilliance. Show the world just how brilliant you are and accept the accolades for it.

As a communicator, the Queen of Wands speaks, not in questions, but in realizations. She shares her inspirations and brilliance as if they have already been realized. She does not leave room for doubt in the possibility of any actuality. In her world, all things are possible, and she expects others to see them that way too. She speaks with authority and knows what she is talking about.

The Queen of Wands may seem lost in her own world, and she probably is in her own world, although it is doubtful that she is lost. The view from her world is unique. It puts her in a position to relate to reality in her own way, which is going to be different from how others approach it. This is her genius, and what makes her a powerful force.

KING OF WANDS

You may not always realize it, but you are influential. People look up to you. You, in a lot of ways, set the tone and the precedence for others to follow. You probably don't even try to do this. It is just the kind of person you are, so it is easy to forget you have such power. This is the King of Wands within you. Realize and appreciate just how much power you have. You don't need to do anything special or go out of your way to be this or that, just be aware and appreciate this piece of yourself.

The King of Wands within you takes itself for granted. He has talents and skills that he has practiced and utilized for so long now that he barely gives any thought to what he is doing. What he does, what sets him apart from other people, he has been doing for so long now that it comes as easily as breathing. These skills and talents are things that other people may struggle with. The King of Wands within you may wonder why they are having such a hard time with it. This piece of you has forgotten what it means to just be starting out at something, as it has long since mastered it. Sometimes, he needs to take a break for a moment and see where others are and how they are doing. He needs to remind himself that not every one has mastered the powers that he himself has. When he does this, he will appreciate the uniqueness of every individual person and maybe see the personal skills they possess that he himself can benefit from.

The King of Wands is a go getter. He sets his goal, and lets nothing get in his way. This draws other people to him. People appreciate the King of Wands for his determination and unwillingness to settle for anything that stands in the way of his objective. He is not one to settle for less. He has the power to visualize the realization of his ambition, and to achieve it. This creates a certain gravity about him. People are naturally drawn to him, as through him, they are inspired to target their own desires and pursue them with equal diligence.

As a communicator, the King of Wands may or may not be completely understood. He may use jargon that he forgets other people may not understand, because they are not at the same level of expertise on a subject that he is. People may need to keep him on the same page as they are so they don't lose track of what he his talking about. This is a minor personality flaw of the King of Wands. All in all, he speaks with passion about the things he is on fire for, and this passion is easily contagious.

The King of Wands is a leader, even if he doesn't care if anybody follows him or not. He just does what he does. He pursues his interests and is a master of his passions. He does this for his own benefit. He does it because to him, it feels right. Whatever good comes from it, that's totally okay and welcomed. Others are welcome to follow. Is this what the King of Wands is necessarily going for though? No. He's just doing what feels right to him, and these are powerful things that don't go unnoticed.

Part Five: Cups

The pieces of ourselves related to our emotions

ACE OF CUPS

The Ace of Cups is that piece within you that experiences joy. It experiences, love, happiness, bliss, and all such manner of uplifting emotions. This piece of you is a container, a literal cup that, when full, gives you the overwhelming sense of well-being. When it runneth over, life is simply as good as it can be. This is the piece of you that walks on air and is in love with life, because life is so good.

What fills your cup? Your cup of joy? Your cup of love? Your cup of happiness? What brings you these emotions more than anything else? The love you feel from others is one such thing that will fill your cup. The love you give is another. When others are receptiveness of what you have to offer, this too fills your cup. A sense of purpose and appreciation go a long way towards filling that cup to the brim. A smooth flow of energy between those around you and harmonious interactions will also keep your cup filled.

When we are happy, we are invincible. We spread our wings and we fly. It is easy. The road ahead is wide open and nothing gets in our way. The path ahead is well illuminated, and the shadows of our fears and doubts are few. If we do find that something is blocking our path, we simply glide over them by the force of our wings with the joy we feel providing the breeze on which we sail.

When you let others know that they are loved, that love will inevitably bounce back to you. The less your own ego needs to be recognized, the stronger that love is. How can love not bounce back to you? When you express love, you open yourself to love. It is inevitable that you will feel it from somewhere in the universe. So express love, but do it in such a way that it is for those you express it to. Don't take the attitude that they owe you something just because you express this to them. Let them respond in a way they feel is appropriate. In this way, love will win. Let love win by not placing expectations on it. Let love be what it is intrinsically.

Imagine that for each emotion you feel, not just love, there is a cup to contain it. What does it feel like to have any of these cups running over? What does it feel for one to be dry? For your cup of happiness or love to overflow, certainly means joy, but an empty cup does not equate to sadness. An empty happiness or love cup brings a feeing of numbness. Sadness comes from a full sadness cup.

The hope is to keep your cups of positive emotions more full than the others. Who and what fills your love cup? To have an empty love cup means to feel numb. It does not mean to feel hate, as hate is not the opposite of love. Indifference is the opposite of love. So to have an empty love cup is to just not care. To feel a strong dislike is to have a full hate cup. Indifference is the lack of love, because even when you feel hatred, there is passion to it, even though the passion is negative. Indifference is the lack of all feelings. When any cup is full, there is no lack.

The Ace of Cups invites you to examine the levels of your different cups and maintain an emotional equilibrium. Even when your cup of joy, happiness, and love are low, don't let that get to you. Accept it as a part of what life is all about. To remain balanced with your head held high even when life has taken a turn towards the negative is to access the power of the Ace of Cups, so ride it out when your sadness cup is more full than your happiness cup. Be comfortable with all your emotions, and see their value.
To be truly dynamic, lean to control your negative emotions. This does not mean to deny them. It means to accept and understand them. It means to funnel them into something constructive, thus turning them into something positive.

Emotions are both compass points and teachers. When feeling a particular emotion, it can be pointing to the direction you don't want to go in. Anger, frustration, resentment, and jealousy are what you try to move away from. Joy, happiness, contentment are what you want to move towards. As teachers, when feeling these things, examine why. What is it about these situations and people that trigger you in this way? Take an honest look at this.

The Ace of Cups is the piece of you that knows the potential of love and yearns for it. It seeks this love, hoping to find it. It plants the seed of this love and hopes it will grow. It remembers this love from divine sources and hopes to find it on the earth.

TWO OF CUPS

The Two of Cups is the piece of you that knows the potential for love and yearns for it. It seeks this love, desiring to find it. It plants the seed of this love with the hopes that it will grow. It remembers this love from divine sources and searches for it on the earth, contained in human physical form.

Imagine your cup of love. Imagine it filled to the brim with the love you feel for another, and the desire to hand it to this person. To pass your love cup to another this way takes courage. It takes strength. It takes hope and faith that they are open to receive it. To do this earnestly, you must be strong and rooted enough to understand and express yourself emotionally. You must know yourself well enough to know what you are looking for in a relationship, as not to get caught up in the dysfunctional partnerships that are the result of rushing into one to fill a gap you have yet to come to terms with.

Now, imagine this person receiving your love cup and treasuring it. Imagine this person handing you his or her love cup in return. The piece of you that can imagine this is the Two of Cups. It is the piece of you that appreciates and honors true, lasting love. It is the piece of you that is a steward of your heart, as well as the caretaker of this other.

Trusting another with your heart, sure that they won't drop it or be careless with it is to sincerely believe that they will take care not to break it or neglect it. This is to be confident they will make sure your love cup stays full to the best of their ability, and be mindful, they trust you to do the same. They are confident that the love they show for you is mutual, and that you will take care not to take it for granted or leave it behind, stopped at a red light that you just ran, or leaving them waiting for you to come home, when you've silently made up your mind you never will. The Two of Cups represents a balanced give and take of love. One genuinely cares about the other, and it is reflected back to them. There is a unity and an honesty to this love. It is not forced or tarnished by the ego and obsessive desires. It is natural and mutually flowing.

To appreciate your inner Two of Cups is to hold one another's cup in perfect balance, carful not to let any of the love contained within splash out or spill carelessly. You treasure the love that is inside your cup, and are honored to receive the cup of another. This love, this give and take of passion, offers a support and understanding that enhances the strengths of your partner and helps them overcome their weaknesses. It is to be a spark of the energy that helps them to shine.

THREE OF CUPS

Imagine that your cup of joy is suddenly full. You had a great experience, a great accomplishment, an important milestone has been reached, or maybe some great news has come your way. You feel good about this. You feel great, in fact, awesome even. You want to share the good feeling. You can't keep it to yourself. It is just too much for you to contain. You're cup of joy is overflowing and you want others to experience your jubilation. This is your inner Three of Cups. It is that piece of you that wants to cerebrate. Celebrating brings others into your success and makes it a shared experience. Celebrations give you cause to focus your attention on what is good and joyful about life.

There is no one set standard for what and how you should celebrate. A celebration can be a big affair, or a small one. Celebrate a personal milestone, like the publication of your first novel, or the promotion you just received. Celebrate the birth of a child. Celebrate getting into the college of your choice. There is no limit to the personal achievements that you can celebrate. Celebrate group accomplishments. Maybe the soccer team you play on won the championship. Maybe the office you work in had a stellar quarter and you want to commemorate the occasion. Don't limit what you celebrate. Pick something that makes you feel good and want to remember, then celebrate it! Celebrate an intimate milestone with a loved one. Is it your wedding anniversary? Celebrate! Live it up! Party!

Celebrations cement special occasions into our consciousness. As time marches on ever into the future and the milestone we have celebrated finds itself farther and farther away from our present moment of the now, a celebration to look back on let's us remember the joy we felt in a concrete way. We will remember the fellowship. We will remember the gathering of friends and people who are important to us. We remember what it was like to be with the important people of our life. We will look at the pictures that were taken and reflect on the words that were spoken, and in our hearts, we will relive the occasion.

Celebrations take us out of our ordinary existence to give us a chance to experience joy with one another. It gives us a chance to focus on a common and shared experience, and an opportunity to appreciate and honor one another. Isn't this an important thing to do? To express appreciation for those in our life? To have bonding moments that bring us together in a sense of oneness? To share the joy of another and to share our joy with them? To celebrate is to appreciate the moments of life and to evaluate them above the mundane. It is to find appreciation for being alive.

You don't always have to wait for a big occasion, if you just want to celebrate. What's wrong with simply cerebrating life? Nothing. That's what's wrong with it. Absolutely nothing. If there is nothing obvious to celebrate, then celebrate something that is not obvious. Celebrate that you have wifi that works. Celebrate the meal you just cooked. Just celebrate. Celebrating reminds us what is good and fun about life, and that life should be that way- good and fun.

Celebrations promote happiness, and when you are happy, the general love of life flows much more easily. In the midst of celebration, love is contagious. As one's heart fills with the love of life, it is felt by the others. This boosts the love that they themselves are feeling. Now all the love that is in the hearts of the celebrants is felt by all, compounding what is already there. This is the Three of Cups piece of you. Celebrate it.

FOUR OF CUPS

In the words of rockabilly superstar, Mojo Nixon, "Buck up and stop your whining." What does he mean by that? He means quit acting like the world is against you. Get over the attitude that the world is here to serve you and if you are not happy for whatever reason, then the world is out to get you. Stop thinking that it is everybody's job to make sure you're happy and content. Lose the attitude that you're the only one who matters. Realize that other people have problems too, and that which you are whining and complaining about is actually pretty petty, all things considered. Stop complaining. Lift your chin up. Look around you. See that there is nothing to cry about. See how silly you are being. That is what he means by it. He could have easily been writing about your inner Four of Cups when he wrote that song.

Quit moping around like the world is out to get you, like the world owes you for this that or whatever else. You do know, don't you, that you are responsible for your own happiness and your own contentment? Don't sit there like everything that is wrong is beyond your ability to fix. Whatever is bothering you is doing so because you are letting it. If you are bored with life, it's because you approach life in a boring way. You create your own paradigms, so if you are discontent with the one you are in, go in and make some changes. Don't expect some other entity beyond yourself to do it for you. The sooner you get this simple idea into your head, the sooner you can start living life to its fullest and stop whining. Do it. Quit whining. Quit complaining. Quit acting like the world owes you something. Lift your head up and realize just how good everything really is when you stop looking at it through the filter of muck and mire of your own making.

If you are in a rut, then do something to get out of it. Ruts happen easily. We get into our daily routines so easily and before we know it, they define us. We become complacent in our routines. We don't even realize how bored with it all we have become until one day it hits us- BAM! Every day is all just the same as every other day. Nothing new is happening, nothing exciting. When this happens, it is seriously time to change things up, however you define that concept. Find something new to do. Do something differently. Create a new routine. If you don't, what do you think you will happen? What could happen is, you will get further and further into your rut and you will become even more bored and maybe even depressed. Don't let this happen! Find ways to make life interesting again.

Boredom can be a self-fulfilling prophecy. We get stuck in the idea that there is "nothing to do" so we sit around and do nothing. When we do this, doom and gloom sets in. We begin to believe the stagnant, empty feeling inside. We begin to believe that this is the true reality of our life. We begin to think that nothing good or worthwhile is going to come around, so we don't try to find anything. We become complacent and willing to do things that bring us very little, if any fulfillment. We accept the unhappiness that this brings. But why? Why do we do this? It makes no sense! Get up! Look around! There is always something to occupy your time and your mind. Quit wallowing in the self-afflicted misery of boredom and look up! Look around! Look behind you! Something is going on somewhere that you can put yourself into. If not, create something. The important thing is, don't sit around feeling sorry for yourself under any circumstances.

FIVE OF CUPS

You can't always get what you want, and things don't always go your way. Sometimes your cups of joy, love, happiness and contentment get knocked over by someone or something, maybe carelessly or maybe on purpose. It happens to all of us, because we all have our sensitivities. We all have those things that bother us. We all have those things that upset us, trigger us, disappoint us, or make us angry. To have these cups knocked over like this and to feel these positive emotions drained is 100% part of being alive as a human being. The Five of Cups piece of you just needs to accept it when it happens. If you can do that, you will thrive on this earth.

You will thrive because you are maintaining control. Negative feelings can easily take over. When you feel them, it is so easy to slip into the patterns they have laid out for you, and play the games they want you to play. Think about it. Your anger expects you to lash out, be destructive, cause damage, and seek revenge. Your disappointment expects you to slip into despondency and stop caring. Your sadness wants you to sulk and hide from the world. What value do any of these actions add to your life? To not give into these feelings and to not react in the way they expect you to is to rise above them. To be above them is to see them from a zoomed out perspective where you can see how they fit into the context of the whole of who you are.

When you are in the middle of these negative feelings, it's easy to only react to them. They are right in front of you, and all around you, so you cannot see what is beyond them. What can you do but react to them? These negative feelings can feel like a fog bank that offers limited visibility. The anger, the sadness, all of it filters your perception of the world to the point that it becomes your world. This is not constructive. It does no good to dwell in such a dark, dank, and negative place. This is why you must rise above them and examine them.

As you examine a feeling that you are experiencing, find what is truly at the heart of it. As you delve into it, you will no doubt find that it is rooted in something that did not go the way you had hoped it would. The lesson here is that sometimes, that's just how it is. You can't always have your own way. You can't expect that everything is going to happen the way you hope it will, and you can't always do anything about that. So accept it. Understand that the world does not bend to meet your needs, and that you are the one who needs to be flexible around the ways of the world.

What do you do with negative feelings when they happen? Do your best to let them pass. Let them pass by not clinging to them. By clinging to a negative emotion, it builds up inside you and stays with you much longer than it should. Acknowledge what makes you feel bad, then shake it off. Move on. Something happened that you couldn't control. Maybe you didn't get a promotion. Maybe your girlfriend or your boyfriend left you. Maybe you were hoping to sell your house, but the buyer backed out at the last minute. Who knows? It could be anything, and it left you feeling bitter.

How long do you plan to keep on feeling this way? Feeling this way doesn't fix anything. Life is how it is, what it is, no matter what you feel about it, so why fixate on what you cannot control? Instead, how about focusing on something you can control? If you do this, you will find yourself feeling better very quickly, because now you are focusing on something positive. Focusing on something positive will take you out of your slump and put you back in top form.

Much of what we feel, be it positive or negative, is based on hopes and expectations. When the expectation is met, it is easy to feel good. When they are not met, we will likely feel bad. When these expectations are based on hopes involving other people and they do not live up to your expectation, it does not mean that it is an attack against you in any way. It just means that they are in a different alignment than you. It's not personal, so do your best to get over it and not make anybody feel guilty about it. Do they deserve a guilt trip over your insecurities? How is that fair? It isn't.

The Five of Cups piece of you is asking you to get over what you feel is against you, because it was never about you to begin with. Nobody is in your head but you. So nobody knows what bothers you but you. So in the course of somebody just going through the moments of their life, don't let it bother you if it seems contrary to wha you want. It's not their fault. Think about it. When things don't go you way, focus on feeling good about what did go your way. There's probably a lot to feel good about, so feel good about these things. Any cups that have been knocked over and spilled, set them back up so that they can be filled again.

SIX OF CUPS

The Six of Cups is that piece of you that remembers the dreams from your childhood. It remembers what it was like to dream and to live in the fantasy that all dreams can and do come true. This piece of you hasn't given up on the idea that wishes, no matter what their relation to reality, can be actualized. Remember what it was like to pretend, and what you fantasized about, at least to you, was 100% real? Remember what it was like to take on other identities, other names, other nationalities, other times, other places, other beings, other species, and to be something completely different from what you are? To live in a completely other skin than the one you were given? This was a time when make-believe became real with a mere thought, because you believed it to be so. This was a time of wonderful empowerment, of strength, and of magic unbound.

You may not consciously remember what it was like to live with such imagination, but your inner child does. Your inner child is your ally. It is your defense against the hum-drum of daily routine. It is your reminder that you don't have to accept life simply as it is thrown at you, but that you can sculpt it and craft it into any form you want it to be. Life is what you make it, so why not make it good? Why settle for less? Why be unhappy? Why be miserable? Why not find the joy in living? The happiness? The sense of optimism that everything is awesome? It's there. Look for it. If you have trouble seeing it, let your inner child show it to you.

Go within and find your inner child and bring it to the surface with you. If you haven't already done so, do it now. Tap into its energy and remind yourself what it is like to feel unlimited. Without limits, all things are possible. So dream as you did as a child. Live without the limitations that reality imposes.

As we grow older, it can happen that we forgot the power of our our dreams. The world gets real as we grow and become older. The notion that we can have anything we want simply by thinking it into being starts to fade away and becomes something that we must rediscover. We get to a point where we must focus on the practical matters of day to day life, leaving little or no time for the games of pretend we could indulge in as children. This is unfortunate.

In these games of pretend, we could decide on an outcome that was the most desirable to us, and live the fantasy of achieving it. It was that easy. As that gives way to reality though, in order to actualize a desirable outcome of an endeavor, we have to focus our energy on the actual work involved in achieving it. We work and work and hope and hope, and cross our fingers that we accomplish what we set out to accomplish. And if we should fall short, then we must find the best in the situation anyway and recalibrate our expectations. We must find what went wrong and tell ourselves it is what we really wanted anyway, or that it was never meant to be. So, endeavor to rediscover that inner child within you that could be who it wanted to be effortlessly.

If your inner child wanted to fly, he or she could fly. If he or she wanted to be a world class race car driver, he or she was a world class race car driver. If he or she wanted to be a surgeon, he or she was a surgeon. What can you learn from your inner child with all this? Learn and remember what it was like to even dare to dream and take on different professions, different personalities, and different identities. By doing that today, you can train yourself to be whatever it is you would like to be, hope to be, wish to be, or plan to be. If you take on the persona of whom you want to become, you can that more easily slide into the skin of who this new you is. Why put it off? Why not go within, find your inner child, and let him or her remind you how to be whatever it is you desire to be? The sooner you do, the quicker you will live as perfectly as you know you can live.

SEVEN OF CUPS

What happens is, we get used to doing things in set and predictable ways. This is fine as long as we expect and are content with set and predictable outcomes. There will be those times though, when we need something else. Or maybe we just crave something else, something new and unique. We need innovation and a new way. In these times, we need to get away from conventionality and look for new ideas. But where do these new ideas come from? How do we find them? What must we do to tap into them and utilize them? These innovations come from the creative and imaginative thoughts found in our explorations of other dimensions.

There is a whole other world to explore. Several whole other worlds, in fact. Actually, there are unlimited other worlds to explore. These are the worlds we find when we push aside our logical mind and put our focus on what is there beyond logic. These are the worlds of possibilities with no limits. These worlds are explored by artists, writers, children, poets, dreamers, innovators, and any and all combinations of such geniuses. In these worlds rules do not apply. In these worlds, there is no God but the god of your own creation.

In these worlds, possibilities are examined, experimented with, and chosen. These are the worlds that can be when the rational mind is forgotten. When we are not bound by what we have been led to believe is reality and what is possible, we are free to believe anything. And when you believe anything, you are bound to try things you ordinarily wouldn't. Somewhere in these trials of impossibilities is the exact right answer you are looking for hiding in plain sight.

When was the last time you let yourself dream and spend time in one of these worlds? The piece of you that is the Seven of Cups knows the value of doing this. It knows that sometimes to find answers, you need to step so far out of the box that you can't even see the box anymore. You need to become so far removed from the box, that you don't even remember there being a box. You need to remove your mind from what is mundane and normal, and step into the realm of the fantastical and unordinary. You need to dream. You need to fantasize. You need to go into a world of make believe where you are not bound by any physical laws or actualities so you can try out these ideas and see how they play out.

Once you have explored these various options, you need to come down to earth and make a solid decision and come up with a solid plan of action. Thinking about doing something doesn't get it done. Doing it gets it done. So don't spend forever thinking about what you are going to do and talking about what you are going to do. Actually do it. Come back down to earth, stand on your own two feet, root in, get grounded, and apply the innovations you found.

You can't expect that everything will take care of itself on its own. No, sticking your head in the clouds to find innovations is only part of the process. You also have to do the work based on what you found. So do that. Put in the work. Make the effort. Get the ball rolling and make things happen. When you do this, you prove to yourself and to the world that you are a genius. You prove that thinking inside of a box is just too limiting for you. You prove what can be done that yes, can be done. And how did you do this? By not accepting limitations.

EIGHT OF CUPS

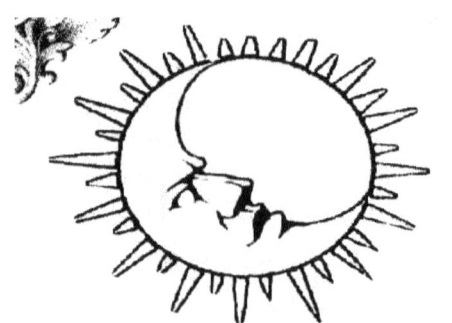

The Eight of Cups within you feels a sense of completion. It feels a sense that you have gotten all you are going to get from a situation, and that no matter what more you put into it, you are not going to get anymore back from it. By the natural order of things, it is just time to move forward and move on.

There is just nothing more in it for you. This is life. This is reality. This is just how things are. It is best to accept it, for in acceptance is the strength to move forward. Denial here is what will slow you down. If you refuse to accept the expiration date of a life situation and experience, you will hold onto it long after it has become stale and repugnant to you. But, if you do accept its completion, life will remain fresh and you will not root yourself into a quagmire.

To grow and to evolve is to recognize what no longer serves us and let it go. It can be tricky sometimes to recognize what these things are. We get so into the flow of our lives that we don't realize or notice how somethings have simply played themselves out. We don't see how our hold on them is hindering our progress towards our own personal evolution and enlightenment. Clinging to what no longer serves a purpose has an unfortunate way of keeping us from intaking anything new that is meant to bring bigger and greater realizations about who we are and what our place in this world and universe is really about. We may or may not even realize the unhappiness this creates.

Think about it. Does it not make us unhappy to cling to something we would so much rather let go of? Does this not initiate the slow deterioration of our happiness until one day we wake up and realize we are miserable? Then we ask, "How did this happen?" We reflect and discover that we can't exactly put our finger on the exact moment our happiness was lost. We realize that a little at a time, we acclimated to the loss of happiness. Then, a little at a time, more of our happiness eroded, and we acclimated to it. Then things kept happening with precious little to fill in the gaps to create new happiness as the existing happiness disappears. So one day, we have an awakening and realize just how unhappy we have become. This is when we realize that if we hope to be happy again, we will need a restart, a reboot, and some big changes.

The best way to achieve these changes, sometimes, is to walk away. Walk away with the acceptance that this once served a purpose to you and was important, and in the "now" that was, it was perfect. But every "now" gives way to the next now and all that this new now has with it. A new now may negate an old now. You may find that the energy of the old now was particularly good for you and it is hard to let go of. But what choice is there if you are going to grow? You must accept change as a natural part of life.

Every now is going to go in its own direction no matter what we want from it. So we leave the old nows behind despite our fondness for them and search for a new now to be excited about. Sometimes this search takes us far, far away. Sometimes it takes us to places we never guessed we'd be, or thought we could ever be. But it is right for us to be there, so that's where we land. We sink our roots into this new now and grow tall within it.

Every now we find our self in has strength to be amassed. We amass that strength and it adds to the totality of who we are. The strength we gain from each now we are in carries over to the next, and to the next, and to the next. No strength gained is ever lost, for it becomes embedded in who we are. So from now to now to now, we continue to grow stronger. This is what it means to journey through life. This is what it means to evolve and to grow. Accept that nothing lasts forever and that change is unavoidable, and you will know what it means to prosper. Deny it and you can expect slow growth, diminished strength, and ultimately, sadness. Your inner Eight of Cups knows when it is best and when to move on. Listen when it speaks.

NINE OF CUPS

The Nine of Cups within you is a very positive, and very powerful force. This is the piece of you that knows great things can happen. It knows that by staying positive, positive things will come to you. The Nine of Cups inside of you is a magnet. It puts out the energy of positivity, and draws more of that to itself, so that even when negativity is present, the negativity does not become the prevalent and dominating force. This piece of you is the creator of miracles. Sometimes it seems like great things happen spontaneously and with unexpected force. This is the power of staying positive and seeing the most favorable outcome of a situation, and understanding the value of patience and clarity, two essential elements of the creation process.

Miracles can and do happen. The Nine of Cups within you knows this. Sometimes, you need to just get out of your own way and let them. You get in your own way when you have doubts. Maybe there is something you really want. This thing, be it tangible or abstract, would make a huge difference to you. But something about it seems impossible and unattainable. It seems too far removed from the realm of possibilities for you to actually have it, so you automatically dismiss the notion that you could ever be yours.

Since you just assume you can never have it, you are blocking the idea that, maybe you can. So stop assuming these things are out of reach. Accept that anything is possible, and everything is within the sphere of actualization. Why limit yourself? Aim high. Aim big. Imagine the greatest, most fantastical outcome for yourself, then dismiss any notions of doubt that say you can't have it. Keep a positive attitude.

Positive attitudes open the window to creation. Negative thinking shuts it. Negative thinking and actions block the flow of creative forces and hinder and altogether stop the process of creation. For this reason, it is best to maintain a positive outlook and disposition even in the face of negativity. The reality of life is that we have negative energy and positive energy. The question becomes, which do we emphasize? To emphasize the positive energy is to tap into the power of creation and new life and of growth. To emphasize the negative is to sink into despair and unhappiness to the point, sometimes, that any positivity and happiness is but a drop in an otherwise empty bucket. While negativity is a reality of our lives, it is a mistake to focus too much energy and thought on it. See it as a reflection of what we would like to change, then endeavor to make these changes.

Put negativity to good use. Get something positive from it. Endeavor to not let it drag you completely down and force you into misery. Find that thing it is telling you needs to be changed, and then change it. When you do this, negativity becomes your friend. You are working in conjunction with it, not in fear or opposition.

When you generate such a powerful atmosphere of positivity, the negativity becomes overshadowed. You are seen and appreciated as a positive person who has many good things in your life. When you stay positive and are seen as a positive person, that which makes your life good is accentuated. The negativity of your life, while still there, is not the primary focus. Because you are so focused on what is good, you are better equipped to handle the negative. When the negative is deemphasized, it almost seems like it is not there. People will notice this about you. They will think that you are somebody for whom great thing always happen. In this way, you are seen as a miracle worker. You are seen as somebody who can accomplish anything. Keep this image alive by maintaining an air of positivity and high hopes.

To create miracles, to create what is seemingly impossible to create, to manifest the true desire of your heart, you must sift through the energy that is present within you, and separate what is positive and what is negative. You must emphasize what feels good to you while not letting the negative sink in. In this way, a positive atmosphere and disposition permeates. When you focus this way on the good in your life, you open yourself to more. In this way, you open the door for miracles.

When creating your own miracles, keep your mind clear and open. When your mind is clear and open, there is no fear or doubt to keep you from achieving your goals and ambitions, and you can accomplish whatever it is that you hope to achieve. In this way, we are the creators of our own miracles. The spark of God within ourselves is activated. With our spark of God activated, we ourselves are God, a part of the collective All that is the Allness of All of the universe, thus rendering ourselves as supremely divine. We need only to recognize this about ourselves to harness that power.

TEN OF CUPS

Where does happiness exist? Happiness exists in contentment. Where does contentment exist? Contentment exists in the feeling that all is well and your well-being is supported. This is to feel appreciated. This is to feel accepted. When you feel accepted, you can relax. You are not worried about fitting in, because you know you fit in. You are not worried about what people think of you, because you know they think well of you. You know you can be yourself without needing to create an image to project, because the person you are is perfectly acceptable and you know this. You don't have to walk on eggshells because people are comfortable around you, and you around them. This sense of collected acceptance and peace is the Ten of Cups within you.

Knowing that those you care about are supported can give you yourself a sense of well-being and support. Your inner Ten of Cups knows this. These people give you a sense of security and appreciation. In this group, all are seen and recognized for their unique abilities and contribution to the group or family dynamics. There is a sense of safety, belonging, trust, and inclusion. There is not a fear of being pushed out or left behind.

This is the example of what a strong family or group and community commitment can be. This is what can be accomplished by genuinely caring about the people in your life and to be concerned with their best interest. This is the accumulation of giving those who are important to you thought and appreciation for what they offer as you yourself strive to be the best person you can be.

In this group, each member feels appreciated and necessary. There is a general sense that nobody will be left behind, and nobody will be forgotten. This is a strong unit where everybody feels safe, and everybody can be who they genuinely are. They are allowed to grow, shift, and change. Everybody is encouraged and nurtured to be the best version of their self. This family, group dynamic generates a synergy that fuels everybody's ambitions and potential.

Your inner Ten of Cups is that piece of yourself that reminds you to be thankful for the people who are always there for you, and for the ones who know you are always there for them. Knowing this support exists leads to ease in life. It leads to ease without the feeling of being taken for granted or taken from. There is a harmonious balance here. This is a nice sense of ease and appreciation for what is good in your life, especially the people who make it that way.

These are the people who support your wellbeing, fuel your ambitions, and give willingly of their selves when you need their power. Maybe you have been feeling down. Maybe you need some cheering up. Maybe the way to feel better is to be open to those who know you best. These are the people who know exactly what it is that will give you the boost you truly need. Maybe these are people you see everyday, or maybe these are people you correspond with from a distance. However these people are in your life, they are your support. They are the ones you can count on, so count on them. Count on them and let them count on you.

There is much to be gained in strong family and group settings. Be open to what they offer you. Allow yourself to grow and to evolve with the support of the people in this group. Give them your love, and accept for yourself theirs. Your inner Ten of Cups has earned this privilege.

PAGE OF CUPS

The Page of Cups is your inner child, sensitive and impressionable. This is the piece of you that is tuned into the emotions of those around you and feels what they are feeling. You share their joys, and you share their sorrows. You feel their anger, and their triumphs. You may not always understand what you are feeling from them, but none the less, you recognize that the emotions you are sensing are coming from them. Even when they attempt to hide their feelings, they do not escape you. Their general disposition is obvious to you, even when nothing is outrightly communicated. You see the truth, even when the truth is shielded, or distorted by dishonesty.

This piece of you is learning what love is. It is learning both how to express it, and how to receive it. It looks to role models, and what it sees, it understands to be the norm. It is learning to understand the inner cups of emotions and what fills them, and what drains them. This is true of their own cups as well as other people's cups. It goes through a period of trial and error as it figures this out, and as it figures out the best way to relate to other people.

Your inner Page of Cups expects to receive compassion as it learns how to show it to others. It is in the process of learning to pick up on cues from others, and to understand what cues get the attention it wants. It is discovering what it takes to get what it needs from others, and how and what to give. It is learning how to love, and is stumbling and making mistakes as it figures out how to fit in, where to fit in, and if it's even worth the effort to try to fit in.

Your inner Page of Cups eventually realizes that everybody is an individual, and has individual needs and expectations as far as relating to them goes. There is no "one size fits all" style for relating to others. While basic understanding and compassion can be universal, the expectations and desires of different people need to be ascertained and respected. Your inner Page of Cups is figuring this out. It has noticed that what works for relating to one person, may not work with others. Just because one person likes hugs and attention, maybe other people don't. Maybe one person likes to have constant attention from others, somebody else may prefer to be left alone. The Page of Cups notices this, and tempers its actions towards people accordingly.

The Page of Cups is sensitive and easily wounded. It places tremendous trust in others and may become disillusioned if that trust is betrayed. This piece of you is prone to hero worship, magnifying a person's good qualities, and will likely put them on a pedestal, only to be disillusioned should they be knocked off and proven to be just like everybody else after all. Because of this, your inner Page of Cups is still in the process of learning. It is learning to be less idealistic and to accept others as they are, and to not take it personally if they do not live up to the glowing and perfect idealization it has of them. The lesson is that we are all humans, and as such, we each have a vast variety of aspects that add up to who we collectively and individually are. To know somebody and to appreciate them is to see and respect even the sides of them that make you uncomfortable.

As a communicator, your inner Page of Cups wants to say the right thing. It wants to say whatever it is that you need to hear. It cares about who it is talking to, and does not want to rock the boat. This piece of you wants its own comfort, and to give comfort as well. Its words will be carefully chosen, and if it feels like it said the wrong thing, it may feel bad about it. This piece of you wants to keep the peace.

Your inner Page of Cups is synonymous with the Fool with a big heart, and because of this, it must be careful. People with good hearts and good souls are often naïve because they see the good in the world. They see the good in people and assume that people see the good in them. Too often though, people only see in these good people what they themselves want to possess and want to take, and so the good people get taken from. Too many times, unfortunately, they don't see that they are being taken from until too much has been taken and now they feel drained.

They sense the loss of what is missing and see that this other person has taken it. Then maybe they beat themselves up for allowing it to happen. They kick themselves for being naïve. They have to realize that this feeling of naiveté is a sign that they are a good person. Somebody who doesn't care at all will not feel this way. They feel this way because they see the good in others, and because they see the good in others, they assume others see the good in them. It comes full circle this way. People who see the good in others are good people themselves. Nobody should kick themselves or beat themselves up for being a good person. Nobody. Good people need to create the space they need to be good people no matter what. This is often a struggle for the piece of you that is the Page of Cups.

KNIGHT OF CUPS

There is a piece of you that is bold in its expression, and idealistic in its relations to others, especially when you want to create an atmosphere of mutual harmony. This piece of you has a perfect vision of how it likes things to be and how it likes to relate to others. It will push these ideas from the core of its being out into the world with the assumption that they will be accepted and understood. When these are well received, this piece of you knows contentment. It knows ease, and it knows satisfaction. When they are not well received, however, this piece of you may take it personally and brood as it heals the wounds these upsets have inflicted. This is your inner Knight of Cups.

As Knights are prone to do, the Knight of Cups charges ahead with its ideas and hopes without slowing down to consider the implications that its actions will have on others. It assumes that the hopes, dreams, and desires it has is shared by everybody around. But are they? The Knight of Cups does not always see right off when they aren't. This causes it grief and frustration. It makes those it interacts with feel like they are being bothered, and harassed. This is a challenge for your inner Knight of Cups. It needs to realize that reactions that are less than they hope for are a part of life, and they are not personal.

The flip side of this is when things go the way the Knight of Cups hopes it will. When your inner Knight of Cups opens its heart to another, and that person appreciates it, it is on top of the world. This is when your Knight of Cups is in its true element. This piece of you is a people pleaser, and to please people makes it feel alive with purpose. It makes it feel better than great. Opening your heart and baring your soul to others, uncertain of how they will respond can be frightening, but if you never face that fear, you will stay stuck in one place and not experience emotional advancement.

Sometimes you just have to take a chance. Not sure how something will work out? Well, don't worry about the outcome. Just put it all out there and see what happens. Shift the paradigm by letting your true feelings be known. Hope for the best, but accept anything that comes of it. Don't just take what comes your way. Do something to generate some sort of an outcome that you would like. How will you know if you don't try? So try! Don't let fear stand in your way. This piece of you lets its heart lead the way, even if it takes it into dangerous territory.

As a communicator, the Knight of Cups within you will risk it all to say what it wants to say. It is often self-centered in that it has its own best interest in mind, even when, by outward appearance, it seems to be offering others what it thinks it needs. And yes, this piece of you does genuinely care for others, but when it comes right down to it, its own self interest is paramount. Its communications with others is often geared towards hearing what it wants to hear.

Your inner Knight of Cups means well, but is not always realistic in its expectations. While good hearted, it can sometimes be overbearing. When it can appreciate others for who they are without trying to force their good nature in any direction or other, this piece of you can be loving and greatly appreciated. When it's trying too hard though, or not getting its own way, it can be unpleasant to be around. This is a fine line it must tread.

QUEEN OF CUPS

The Queen of Cups within you cares about other people so much it hurts. It wants the ideal perfection for others and will sacrifice and do whatever it takes on their behalf to help them achieve it. This is a mothering piece of you. As a mother would care for and protect its young, so too do you care about the people who are important to you. This piece of you is sensitive to the needs of others, and will do anything for them. It is inclined toward unconditional love.

The Queen of Cups is essentially the Empress whose heart is open to others. Just as the Empress expresses her mothering qualities to the earth, the Queen of Cups has its heart open to those who need it and those it has chosen to take into her care. Caring for others and showing them compassion is second nature to her. When it sees somebody who needs what it has to offer, it gives it to them. Simple as that. She does not ask for or expect anything in return. She gives because those she gives to have needs.

As the Queen of Cups gives what is needed, it must assess what that is, and it's not always perfect joy, sweetness, and happiness. Sometimes it is a reality check. Sometimes others need a brutal reflection of who they are, or who they are becoming. It happens that people begin making bad decisions. They fall under the influence of elements that bring them into a bad state of being. The Queen of Cups sees this. She knows that this person is going down a destructive path, and without intervention, it is only going to get worse for them. So she steps in.

She becomes the voice of reason or the voice of authority that says, "Knock it off!" This is tough love. This is to make herself unpopular or unliked in the eyes of who it is helping, but not caring about that. The attitude is, "This person needs help, and I'm going to give it to them no matter what. They may not like me now, but they will thank me later." And letting it go at that.

As a communicator, your inner Queen of Cups is adaptable. While she appreciates honesty, she may temper the message she is sending with just the right amount of what the person with whom she is communicating needs to hear. What this person needs to hear may not be completely rooted in reality, but a degree of hopeful suggestions and positive thoughts will go a long way towards helping them find the inspiration they need to achieve their goals. The Queen of Cups finds just the right words to say.

The Queen of Cups appreciates the perfection of all beings. She sees in them all, the potential they have for greatness. She wants to nurture that. She wants to coax that greatness to the surface. To do this she offers encouragement. She offers resources, and she offers the space they need and the time necessary. When your inner Queen of Cups sees those she cares about achieve their perfection, she too feels victorious.

KING OF CUPS

You may see somebody in pain dealing with some personal issue, and have compassion for them, recognizing and seeing your self reflected in their pain. Because you understand their pain it can easily happen that you are glad that it is not you going through it this time. Your attitude may be, "Good. It's not just me to go through this. Why should I be the only one? If I can get through it, so can they." You might even take the attitude, "Why are they taking it so hard? When I went through that, I handled it much better than they are. What's their problem anyway? They need to just get over it. I did." It is so very easy to project your standards and attitudes into the pain others are experiencing.

Your experience, it seems, makes you an expert in what others are going through. You can though, turn this into healing compassion for this person. It is possible to send them healing energy and understanding. Remember the feeling and sensation of being healed of this pain. Capture that feeling. Hold it as energy. Infuse this energy with divine love and power. Now visualize that energy going into this other person and filling first their heart center, and then radiating out to the rest of their being until they are filled with the healing energy. The ability to do this is the true power of the King of Cups.

The King of Cups piece of you wasn't born, it was created. It has grown into what it is. It wasn't always this way, it became what it is through a lifetime of pain, healing, and growth. It became what is through a lifetime of joy, happiness, and analysis. In other words, this piece of you has been through it all, it has seen it all, and it has experienced it all. And all of this was not for nothing. No, every bit of it has been a growth experience and a chance to learn and understand what each emotion is, what triggers them, and what can be gained and learned from them each. It does this to understand its own self, and what it learns, it sees also in others.

What it learns is not just for its own sake of knowing. What it learns is transmuted into compassion for others. It becomes understanding for what another is dealing with or going through. It also becomes a caring voice and helping figure that can offer guidance through the difficult patch another is going through. It becomes the sage advice and knowledgeable wisdom that they can count on. It becomes the father figure that shows the way. It becomes the voice that says, "I know what you are going through. I've been through it myself. Let me help you."

The communication style of your inner King of Cups is kind and compassionate. It is understanding as well as knowledgeable. It is not out to judge, but rather to understand. It seeks to understand the inner workings of its fellow humans in order to learn about them, to ascertain where they are emotionally and spiritually. It is there to offer guidance and support.

The King of Cups within you is essentially the Magician with a compassionate heart. He seeks to understand what is the truth of himself and of whom he encounters, and to foster an air of understanding based on what he learns. He seeks to know how others feel so that he may manifest whatever healing energy and understanding they require. The piece of you that iis the King of Cups genuinely cares about others and wants to offer guidance when he can.

Conclusion

I hope that by reading this book, your eyes were opened not just to the multitude of aspects of yourself and others, but to the idea that you have absolute free will to craft the you that you would like to be. While there are pieces of yourself that are intrinsic to your life's mission, it is completely possible to choose who you would like to become. If you have discovered that you appreciate the characteristics of any particular archetype, but do not feel you posses them strongly, you now know what to concentrate on to gain those qualities. Take King of Cups for example.

The King of Cups posses the incredible ability to feel empathy and appreciation of others. He can see into people what they are feeling, and what they need to be completely content. Is this a quality that you would like to develop for yourself? If so, practice listening to others. Practice observing them. Do your best to imagine what they are thinking, and what they are feeling. Project yourself into their worldview and imagine how it must feel to experience the sensations of the world as if you were them.

Once you have this fixed in your mind, examine what you would do if you were in their skin. How would you seek perfection of life based on the paradigm you have created by you perception of them? From this, feel compassion. Develop empathy. Offer the best advice you have. This is to be of benefit to the world as the King of Cups.

Consider the qualities of any archetype you wish to strengthen within yourself. To be a stronger leader and develop a more authoritative voice, focus on enhancing your Emperor qualities. To accept the inevitability of change and the appreciation that not everything we think is important actually is, focus on developing your inner Tower. To develop patience and an understanding that everything, no matter what, takes the time it needs to become actualized, accentuate the Seven of Pentacles within you. Meditate on any of the archetypes you wish to develop, and before long, you have awakened them and now they will grow, offering you their strength.

Whoever you discover yourself to be, appreciate being that person, for this is who you are. This is tarot in its rawest, truest power. This is to strip away the trappings and expectations of a traditional tarot card reading, and get down to the primordial functions of each card. This is to know yourself on a soul and spiritual level. May what you discover give you power.

Also By Jim Larsen

What's Tarot Got To Do With It? The Fool's Path to Enlightenment

The Double Oh Fool Guide to Tarot Mastery

Knowings From The Silence: Simple Wisdom for an Enlightened Life vol. 1-4

Fat Naked Poetry

www.ingramcontent.com/pod-product-compliance
Lightning Source LLC
Chambersburg PA
CBHW071458070426
42452CB00041B/1909